CREATING A
GARDEN

MARY KEEN

CREATING A

GARDEN

Special photography by Andrew Lawson

conran
OCTOPUS

To my family

First published in Great Britain in 1996 by
Conran Octopus Limited
37 Shelton Street
London WC2H 9HN

Reprinted 1997

British Library Cataloguing-in-Publication Data
A catalogue record for this book is available from
the British Library.

ISBN 1-85029-719-3

Commissioning Editor: Sarah Pearce
Project Editor: Stuart Cooper
Copy Editor: Sarah Riddell
Editorial Assistant: Helen Woodhall

Art Editor: Leslie Harrington
Visualizer: Lesley Craig
Illustrators: Vanessa Luff, Liz Pepperell,
Corinne Renow-Clarke

Picture Research: Jess Walton
Production: Julia Golding
Index: Hilary Bird

Produced by Mandarin Book Production
Printed and bound in China

CONTENTS

PREFACE

Being given the chance to design the gardens around the new Opera House at Glyndebourne was wonderful, but the gardens I love best are on a much more intimate scale.

Some gardens are paradise, with an emotional charge which lifts the spirits. These are private territory, a map of associations and dreams, and a safe haven from the world. Modern expectations demand a product, a finished work, but an instant design will rarely turn into a place that haunts the memory. Layouts and planting plans are only the start, because no garden is ever made: it is the process, the making, that matters. In time, even the smallest plots acquire layers of meaning. We are talking intangibles here. Atmosphere, peace, the chance to experience a garden in the long light of dawn, or the glimmer of dusk, is elusive. For those who want to learn how to grow and group plants, visits to other gardens are useful, but in such crowded places, peace never comes dropping slow. The objective experience, with the garden observed, is not the same as the subjective association, which is only to be found in the garden that you work in yourself. With the garden that you look at, the relationship is superficial; with the one that is part of your life, commitment can be total.

When I make gardens for other people, I am involved in a long search for the connection between the owner and the place. It has to be what the client wants it to be, within horticultural bounds, and it has to belong to the place. Sometimes these demands are hard to reconcile. Many of the gardens where I have helped are large and often the point of them is display: they are for showing off to friends or visitors. They tend too to be places where the owners do not garden. I enjoy the work, and the chance to carry out lavish schemes, but most of the gardens that I like best are smaller. These are the ones where the owner, or a thoughtful gardener, is deeply involved with the day-to-day management. Gardens with soul need an animator who will breathe life into their being, and who responds to the resonance of a particular place. Otherwise they slip back into insignificance. 'Beautifully maintained' is not the same as 'lovingly managed'. If it is a chore and not a pleasure it will show.

There is a bewildering array of advice on gardens and design and another leap into print is hardly justifiable. However, when my oldest daughter embarked on garden making, she wanted to know how I started and what I thought about. Over the last three years, since we moved here to begin all over again, I found that the way I tackled this garden was very different from the way in which I develop designs for others. It seems exclusive to concentrate on one particular site, but it would have been hard to explain the thought processes involved in more general terms. Getting under the skin of a place is what matters. It is much easier to do this when working on one's own patch than it is for other people. Designers can help to organise the work and suggest techniques for building a garden. They can also produce plenty of ideas, but they will never be better at understanding a place than the person who lives there. Nobody will design a more satisfying garden for you than the one that you think out for yourself. It could take years, but in the doing of it, you should be, as we have been, in paradise.

PLAN OF THE GARDEN

Garden Rooms

1 The Dell and the Pool

2 The Summer and Winter Garden

3 The Hellebore Beds

4 The Terrace

5 The Orchard

6 The Gooseberry Garden

7 The Kitchen Garden

Buildings

8 The house and sheds

9 The woodshed/garage

10 The schoolroom and glasshouse

11 The church

Major Trees

12 Yew

13 Copper beech

14 Chestnut

15 Apples

16 Cedar

17 Lime

0   5m   10m

0   10ft   20ft   30ft

N

PART ONE:
THE STORY OF A GARDEN

THE NEW GARDEN

Finding the spirit of the place • House and landscape •
History and the present • Unity of purpose •
A place to be • Clearing views • Moving in

The best way to make a garden is slowly. When I work for other people, decisions have to be taken much faster than I would like: the sight of the consultant walking round the garden just 'getting the feel of the place' inspires no confidence in the client. The recommendation of Pope, the poet and eighteenth-century gardener, to 'consult the genius of the place' is still the best advice to any garden-maker.

Sometimes, as it was with our new house, the genius is hard to find. The place was certainly beautiful. House-hunting on an October afternoon, I drove down a narrow valley where beech woods hung above a small stream to find a tall house covered in Virginia creeper and surrounded by dusty evergreens. It was a disappointing conclusion.

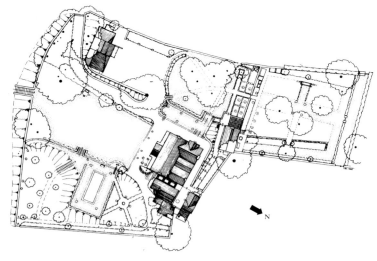

LEFT: *Once the Virginia creeper had been removed, the cars banished from the front*
of the house and the porch restored, the place looked less daunting.

Even before plants began to grow, the table and chairs in the sun provided a resting place. The freshly limed porch gable still lacks a rose, but the gravel terrace soon became a home for thymes and self-seeded hollyhocks and mulleins.

But behind the three-storey building – and dwarfed by it – was a Saxon church. 'You must see it. It is Chaucer's England,' wrote John Betjeman in a letter to a friend. In his *Guide to Parish Churches of England and Wales* he described it as 'an enchanting place' and gave it a star for being an exceptionally attractive church. Of course, say friends, you fell in love with it all at first sight, but it has to be admitted that, unlike Capability Brown, I failed to see that the place had any capabilities of improvement. However beautiful the valley and the church, the house was daunting and the garden non-existent.

Faced with growing flowers where the climate seemed cold, the gradients steep and the soil stony, I found it hard not to question the fact that the Cotswolds are famous for their gardens. Our last house was on a gentle south-facing slope. The gravelly soil drained fast, and it was easy to work and around the house it was always warm. Abutilons often lasted through the winter in Berkshire; there was a 3-metre-tall bay tree and we pruned our roses before Christmas. In the Cotswolds, the accepted principles seemed to be quite different. Gardening looked like much harder work and the wind was clearly a problem. Locals implied that snow fell every winter. Love at first sight it was not, but there was nothing else on offer. We had sold our house in the favoured Berkshire plot, so because the surroundings and the church were irresistible we decided to take it on. Privately, I was dismayed by the prospect.

The valley was beautiful enough, but the house did not seem to belong to it. From the front, there were no views out to connect it with the landscape. Nor were there any plants to suggest local distinctiveness. Heathers and hypericum covered a steep bank to the west, indicating a hasty visit to the garden centre. At the back of the house, instead of Cotswold stone, machine-extruded concrete slabs and walling created one side of an artificial rockery, where more heather grew. A bright blue swimming pool lay uncomfortably near the boundary wall. Meanwhile the house had to be re-roofed and major restoration works were being carried out indoors. Tiles, scaffolding, lorries and skips surrounded the building and the noise of transistors and hammers filled the air. Buried in an inappropriate setting and drowned by the noise of building works, it was hard to know where to start. Textbooks recommend a year of waiting to see what will appear in a new garden, but that seemed much too long. I began to worry that if we did not make a garden soon I would turn against the project.

Taking the Virginia creeper off the house was a help. It revealed a pearly grey stone ashlar front with Georgian windows that cried out for space around the building. Using the house as a source of inspiration often provides the key to making a garden. Much of the work that I do for other people surrounds old buildings, and the architecture usually governs what happens between the house and the landscape beyond. It sounds exclusive to say that all gardens are a link between man and nature when some people have to live in towns, but towns have landscapes too and the trees in a street or in a neighbour's garden form the surroundings that enclose the smaller scale of the private plot. Where there is a dominating street tree, a row of cherries perhaps, then planting something that complements what is already there will work better than fighting back with a solo specimen on your particular patch: it is the sense of belonging to the house and to its environment that makes a garden work for me. However attractive a feature, if it does not fit with the mood of the building or the landscape around it, then it cannot be allowed. It is knowing what to leave out that gives a garden unity.

Once the house presented a clean face to the world I began to appreciate what sort of a place it was and to learn something about its history. In 1805 the Rectory was described in a survey of its buildings by Corpus Christi College of Oxford, which owned the parish, as 'dilapidated and inhabited by a labourer'. In 1834 the Rector had rebuilt it, giving it the façade of a doll's house. It was the sort of house that would always have had a neat view of glebe fields, with perhaps a shrubbery walk and flower beds filled with well-grown plants, as well as a kitchen garden. A hundred years later the place had been sold to an architect, Sidney Gambier-Parry, who, in the early 1920s, added a gabled Cotswold-style elevation and an Arts and Crafts porch to the front door. He kept bees and restored the church and probably planted the thujas that had become a massive presence in the garden by the time we bought the house. He was followed by the sister of Katherine Mansfield, the writer. She had a collection of hellebores that was enviable and cherry trees that produced baskets

The presiding genius of the place is the ancient small church, seen through the door in the wall below the hellebore beds.

13

The first sight of the house was unpromising. Compare the dark crowded space on the left with the open feeling created by the new terraces shown on pages 10–11. Virginia creeper is rarely an adornment on a south-facing wall.

of fruit. She loved the place and those who had met her spoke of her energy and her goodness. There was little left of her garden. No hellebores remained and the cherries had gone, but there was a bed of lilies-of-the-valley under one of the sheds and a spectacular red tree peony which had seeded itself in several places. Immediately before us, the house had been lived in by a family who also fell under the spell of the church and they kept the garden remarkably tidy: there were hardly any weeds. But swayed by modern fashion, they had introduced the man-made building materials and the easy-care shrubs that seemed out of keeping in a place with so much history. There is nothing wrong with modern materials and plants, but they work better in modern settings.

Gradually, a picture of the sort of garden that the house needed began to emerge. Something of its early nineteenth-century outlook over what were once glebe fields should be restored. These no longer went with the house, but sheep still grazed their grass. It should have something of the Arts and Crafts spirit that is so strong around these parts and which Gambier-Parry had practised in the house. That meant using local

materials and good craftsmanship, which never comes cheap, but if we had to wait years to do it properly then years it had to be. Some might find this Arts and Crafts element in conflict with the Georgian house. Purists dislike the porch which sticks out over the door. But it was there, and for me it is part of a strong local tradition and saves the house from looking too bland and predictable. At the back, the building is gabled and much older. This is Cotswold vernacular style. It could have been ignored and the place made to look more like a miniature version of a grand house, but the rooms inside are small square parlours. In scale it is the same size as the house which became the home of the Dashwoods, when they fell on hard times in *Sense and Sensibility*: Jane Austen called that a cottage. It had to belong, too, to the much older tradition of the church. The tiny humble building behind the house made dreams of grandeur quite out of place.

Setting up guidelines that are influenced by the style and setting of the house has never prevented anyone from having the garden they want. For most of us, the basic needs are somewhere to sit and a corner for flowers. If these simple wants have a

When we came there was no view of open fields and sheep grazing. The lawn was a small enclosed space crowded at the edges by the large thuja hedge on one side and a phalanx of firs and laurels on the other.

In the kitchen garden, daffodils appeared as we moved in. The larger golden ones are modern additions, now removed to make way for those of gentler colour. On one of the apple trees in the foreground it was a thrill to find sprouts of mistletoe.

unifying theme, the garden, however small, will be a satisfying place. Larger gardens provide the chance to grow vegetables, somewhere for children to play and a utility area for rubbish and compost, as well as several different sites for plants. Those who love flowers might want both sunny and shady situations, or might like, as I do, to keep separate areas for different seasons. However much space any gardener has, there is never enough to grow all the plants on offer. The temptation is always to try to fit in everything seen or read about until there is no more room. Respecting some unity of purpose is not a hindrance: by imposing discipline it distils the effect of the garden and so creates more than just a collection of plants. It also transforms a garden into a place to be, rather than one that is there just to be looked at.

In the early stages of planning, it helps to imagine a route: a selfish walk, with plenty of stops, that might happen with a companion who also loves gardens, but more often is taken alone. For me, the best gardens are places for losing myself and this was what I most wanted for our own garden. It was never intended for groups of garden visitors who collect around rare plants or examine colour combinations; these will always be, I think, secondary to the spirit of the place, and to the concept of the garden.

The best aspect of the house was spoiled by a gravel sweep in front of the south-facing windows and the look-out over the pocket-handkerchief lawn was darkened by too much overgrowth. Facing east, a 30-metre hedge of thuja stretched along one side of the grass and there was a dense shrubbery to the south. On the western edge a couple of ragged cypresses appeared above a hedge of spotted laurel and lilac. The tall house was hemmed in on all sides. It had to be given air and light around it. Le Nôtre, the architect who worked for Louis XIV at Versailles, said that every house should have a terrace as deep as the building was high. It is not a bad rule, but nothing so formal as a terrace is needed. A length of lawn in front of a house produces the calm setting that improves every building. Le Nôtre laid out hard surfaced terraces for people to walk about in comfort, with no risk of wet shoes, but for modern living grass is just as good. Our ancestors' social life was conducted while walking; today we prefer to lie on the grass to talk or use the lawn for playing games. This level space in front of the house also acts as an anchor. It settles the building into its surroundings, and for those who sit or lie around in front of it the solid presence is reassuring. To create a lawn in front of our new house, the cars had to be condemned to park near the garage. Although it is a nuisance to have to walk several metres in the rain with a box of groceries, I would always try to ban cars from the area around the house if at all possible, because it invariably improves the setting.

To increase the feeling of space we enlarged the lawn by removing the thuja hedge. It turned out to be surface rooting, so it was not a serious task. The hedge and the cypresses were felled by a local tree surgeon, who left us a mountain of home-grown bark that came in useful for mulching. The money was well spent. We uprooted the lilacs and snowberry on the southern boundary ourselves and, after stones had been picked up and grass sown, we looked forward to a respectable lawn and a view of sheep grazing on a green hill. The setting of the house was transformed.

Clearance on a major scale is nerve-racking and involves much peering out of high windows to see what you might see if the view were clear. The enormous thuja hedge did conceal much of our neighbour's farmyard, but it also hid a beautiful wood. Replaced

From the landing window in autumn there is a view of the lawn and the misty hill beyond.

by yew, the new hedge would, in time and with plenty of dried blood, edit out the mechanical aspects of the farming and allow us to see the wood. With encouragement, it now grows 30 centimetres a year; those who groan at the slowness of yew as a hedging plant have never used dried blood as a fertilizer.

To the west of the house, we inherited a small orchard sloping to a pair of rose beds filled with Hybrid Teas. Below that, the slope continued with the bank of heather and hypericum, to a high wall that came depressingly near to the windows. Like the front, the western side lacked space. Terracing would change the claustrophobic bank into ordered levels and give the building the room it so badly needed. It was the second area that we tackled, with the help of a local dry-stone waller. Two walls replaced the one tall one. A height of just over 1 metre near the house is much more acceptable, and the upper wall, which retains the orchard and the site of the rose beds, became slightly taller. Between the two walls we made a level terrace.

In the spring of that first year (we moved in March), making the terraces and bones of the garden above and to the west of the house was a priority, but no substitute for gardening. We could not spend a year deprived of growing things. In the kitchen garden under the church tower, we found orchard trees and the legacy of a chicken-run. There were two small beds dug out for vegetables. Here we dug out more grass, in order to heel in the plants that we had brought from our old house to our new life. Officially, everything in the garden that is left behind is classed as a fixture. Like the curtain rails and light fittings, plants may not be removed. The difference is that, unlike the fixtures and fittings indoors, most things outside can be cloned. For our spring start we had begun planning and propagating in Berkshire the previous summer. Long before the old house was sold, various named hellebores had been lifted and replaced with plants of lesser rarity, on the grounds that it would be an unlikely buyer who could tell the difference between *Helleborus* x *nigercors* and the ordinary *H.* x *argutifolius*. If anyone had come along with an appetite for the best forms of hellebore, I would have been so delighted to leave them in good hands that they could have been returned to their homes. But such a connoisseur never emerged, so the rare hellebores went into the furniture van. There were, too, the sentimental plants, the gifts from other gardeners. A particularly good form of pulmonaria, the hebe achieved from a

The greenhouse, stained grey-brown, was designed to provide a home for climbing pelargoniums and plumbago as well as a working area where cuttings and tender plants could overwinter. After they were first cut back, the yew trees above the bank looked as though they might never grow again, but after three years they could be turned into respectable topiary shapes. (See page 84.)

cutting taken from a bunch of church flowers long past their best, the rose first seen on an Italian holiday – none of these could be left behind. Associations are just as much a part of gardening as flowers. Banksian roses can be bought, but they will never be the same as the one grown from a cutting brought home from Italy. The daphne grown from seed given away by a famous gardener might be smaller than the same form sold in a garden centre, but its provenance will always make it a more interesting plant. The tricky, the rare and the sentimental all made the journey from the old garden to the new. Looking after them in that first dry summer kept us busy and provided the continuity that was needed to make it seem as though gardening had not stopped.

Some plants went into permanent quarters around the house. On either side of the path that ran upwards along the back of the house, pulmonarias and hellebores were planted for an immediate spring tonic. Later, at the front of the house, summer beds were made for half-hardy plants like the blue mallow and chocolate red cosmos, under annual climbers of white cobaea, golden eccremocarpus and blue morning glory. In spite of the stony unprepared soil, which was full of bindweed and ground elder, a few vegetables were grown. Working outside in these areas, which were beginning to seem like our own, a picture of the sort of garden that might emerge began to take shape. Spending long hours outside helps the creative process. Even the most ordinary tasks,

Behind the house, the hellebores and early spring flowers were planted. This photograph shows only two steps on the long gravel slope and a line of roof tiles edging the bed. Two more stone steps were added later and large lumps of local stone used to mark the path.

like raking leaves or weeding, can prompt the mental involvement in a garden. Almost as though you are plugging in to an electric current, you begin to be charged with its moving spirit and you discover things no plan can ever reveal. It is often only after you have passed the same place for weeks that you realize there is something special about it. It might be a sheltered spot to sit out of the wind, a view of a neighbouring tree or a corner which the evening sun always catches, but until you have spent time absorbing the details of a place you cannot know what is right for it. The feeling around the house, and of what grew in the area locally, sank in slowly over the first summer. On old farmhouses nearby, golden ivy or deep crimson roses grew. In the brick houses where we had previously lived, yellow and red had been difficult colours to place, but against a stone background I learnt to appreciate them more than the white or pale pink which had been my standby in our last garden. On the gable end of a house in a neighbouring village there was nothing but a huge fan-trained pear. That, in its simplicity, was an

Looking back at the house from the farm below, it is impossible to see the lane beneath the high wall and the steps that end our lawn. From the front door, clearing the view revealed an old blue tractor parked on a slope so that it would always start. For some this might wreck the idyllic valley scene but we enjoy the sight of the tractor just as much as that of the horses.

inspiration. Stone walls sprouted valerian, and snowdrops were everywhere, on roadside verges and in the local woods. Cowslips grew on the north-facing slopes of sheep-grazed fields and in summer black mulleins with yellow flowers appeared, followed by meadow cranesbills along the valley road under the roses and honeysuckle that sprouted from the thorn hedge. Ladies' bedstraw, orchids, lilies-of-the-valley and hellebores could all be found growing nearby. It was very different from Berkshire; the landscape seemed more ancient, less disturbed, and if the garden were to belong to it, that local distinctiveness would be an important feature.

Noticing what grows well around a new garden is all part of consulting the spirit of the place. Local buildings, the lie of the land, the trees and smaller plants are always signs of the prevailing genius. By the end of the first year it was decided that we would try to make a Cotswold garden, with a sense of timelessness and of belonging to the landscape and to the ancient church behind the house.

THE GOOSEBERRY GARDEN

Poor man's vistas • Moving oil tanks and mulberries •
Box hedges • Fruit and herbs • An orange-and-blue colour
scheme • A simple larch pergola • A modern inscription

A chance to stage the ascent to an eye-catching view or object is every garden designer's dream. Much of this garden is linear and steep, so the potential for surprises to crown all our horizons was huge. If you have to walk through a garden roughly in a straight line uphill, you need something to look at in the middle distance as you walk. Grand gardens can lead the eye into enclosures which open out into friendly spaces that surround you with plants, or to gates that open on to beautiful landscapes. Where there is less room, it helps to focus the eye on an object or a plant; a pot, perhaps, or a tree.

One of the first areas that we tackled was the route from the back door up a stepped path between the narrow beds that we now call the hellebore beds. The path skirts a

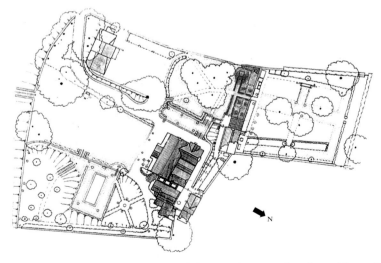

LEFT: *The view towards the arbour at the corner of the gooseberry garden shows blues of borage and delphiniums in the background, violas and strawberries to the fore.*

ABOVE: *The mulberry tree ends the long upward path less formally than an ornament would.*

BELOW: *The bones of the garden stand out in winter and early spring.*

small building that used to house the village school for all of six pupils, and passes the greenhouse, still rising, until the line straightens out for the last 18 metres to the boundary wall, just beyond the turning into the kitchen garden. At the top, the view that we inherited was of a huge thuja blocking the wall, flanked by a battleship of an oil tank that occupied the angle where two walls meet. The evergreen was a favourite with gardeners at the turn of the century and must have been planted with the best of intentions as an eyecatcher at the end of the path. At 21 metres, it was now out of scale with its surroundings and for me was too dominating a presence in what should have been a domestic and sunny part of the garden. To the right of the path was our only south-facing wall and to the left the small orchard with five picture-book apple trees. The early twentieth-century owner, Sidney Gambier-Parry, who planted the thuja, had also planted an incense cedar and two Norway spruces to line the route, on the orchard side of the path, which were stealing the sun from the best planting place. Nor did they seem right as neighbours for apple trees. It was clear they had to go, but because this is a conservation area, planning permission was needed. Once that had been given, on the promise that we would plant another tree in place of the thuja, all the conifers were felled by a good tree surgeon, who ground out the stumps and branches, leaving us with a pile of coarse woodchip to spread on the garden.

The chosen tree for the sight line up the long path was a black mulberry, about 4 metres high with a spread of 3 metres. We brought it from our last garden because black mulberries are scarce and slow to grow. So when we moved, we reserved the right to take the tree. Uprooting anything that size is risky. The first summer here was hot and, in spite of repeated waterings, there was not a leaf to be seen on our mulberry. In June, a knowledgeable gardener suggested that only a thrice-daily shower could save its life, so morning, noon and night the twiggy wood was sprayed until six weeks later we were rewarded with tiny green leaves.

One tree does not a vista make and the oil tank was still a formidable presence in the corner. Moving tanks is expensive work, however, and I agreed to live with it and put up some wattle hurdles to hide its bulk while planning what to do with the space between the path and the south wall. The previous owners had tended a narrow bed under the wall where a few roses and some delphiniums grew with a patch of turf in front, and the whole area measured about 4 metres wide by 6 metres long. One solution that would have appealed to gardeners who put plants first would have been to make a wider border against the south wall filled with sun-loving flowers; 4 metres is not too wide for a mixed border of shrubs and perennials. But the feeling of the old apple trees in the orchard on the other side of the path would have been dispersed by a large bed

filled with half-hardy plants and bright flowers. It seemed better to reinforce the orchard/kitchen-garden atmosphere, rather than to introduce a planting that was not part of that picture. It was not just that I thought the plants would be inappropriate, but their scale would have been wrong. It was as though I were painting a Beatrix-Potter-sized watercolour and someone had come along and said, 'You ought to put some big strokes of oil paint in that corner to brighten it up a bit.' In all the gardens where I work, I try to be consistent about sticking to one idea at a time and going with the dominant theme of the place. The apple trees had it. It was a pity to forgo the chance of growing *Buddleja crispa* and trachelospermum on the wall, with a range of salvias and roses in the bed below, but if you fight the spirit of a place you always lose.

If the south wall was not to be used for exotic flowers, it was not going to be wasted. The kitchen garden beyond it is walled on only three sides and where the south wall ought to be there is a hedge, so there were no possibilities of figs or peaches there. The obvious place for fruit was on the wall facing the orchard, and it could also occupy the space between the wall and the path. A little fruit garden with salads and herbs, plenty of marigolds and borage and nasturtiums would be quite in keeping with the orchard and would lead logically into the kitchen garden. But to make sense it needed to be linked with the orchard in some way and yet separated from it. Low box hedges are

Late in the season, the rich oranges and brown of sunflowers and marigolds replace the pale yellows and blues that appear before midsummer.

traditional in old kitchen gardens, and in modern potagers dwarf box marks out the plots. At Hinton Ampner in Hampshire, now the property of the National Trust, I had seen and admired an unusual way of using box as a surround to an orchard of apple trees in long grass. If the edge of the path that bordered the orchard was lined with box and the fruit garden was surrounded by it, the two areas would look as though they belonged together. The box would also help the look of the path, which had to be hard for practical reasons. Grass paths are nice, but not on slopes that are used every day in winter, and stone we could not have afforded. Gravel would have been hard to manage on a slope, and concrete is too alien to be beautiful, so crushed limestone or local hoggin was used to make a dry route all the way from the back door to the kitchen garden. Edged now with box and ending in a view of the mulberry, it began to look as though it had been there for ever. The 'as-found' look, rather than something that looks fresh off the designer's page, is what works best for me, perhaps because I tend to work with gardens that surround older houses.

The box (*Buxus sempervirens*) is intended to grow to knee height. Any thing shorter would look silly around the orchard, but the fruit garden was going to need some quite strong features if it was to hold its own behind the dark green hedge. An area of 6 metres by 4 metres is too big to plant with low-growing things.

Dividing the space with crossing paths for a quartered effect would help to break up the space and reduce the scale of the bed as well as making it possible to walk among the plants, but proper paths were not in the spirit of the place. Stepping stones in a sea of

ABOVE: Viola *'Arkwright's Ruby' appears early in the season with geum and veronica. The gooseberry garden is too hot and dry for violas to survive the summer, but they always seed themselves lavishly for the following year.*

BELOW: *The reliable blue iris 'Jane Phillips' has leaves which last well after the flowers have faded.*

green were more what I wanted. It is at this stage, at the fine tuning of a patch of ground, that decisions become harder. If the box hedges had been neater and smaller and I had allowed them to line crossing paths of solid stone or brick, the feel of the garden would have been much smarter. I admire modern potagers in the French neo-Renaissance Villandry mould, but they are too sophisticated for this place. Their maintenance is crisper than I can manage and smart gardens need settings to match.

The stepping stones were lying around in the garden. We had to find them large enough for a generous footprint and thick enough not to crack when walked upon. They were laid level, on a little sand and grit with no mortar. For the paths that ran into the wall, more stepping stones would have been acceptable, but too many of them might have tipped the balance towards the understated and improvised. We were lucky. Several staddle stones – those stone mushrooms that farmers used to put under barns to keep the rats away – were ranged along the lawn, rather unhappily out of a job. As bygones, reminders of their rat-preventing past, I never much like them, but the upside-down tops made wonderful round stepping stones and the bases were used for steps and bollards where we needed them. The arrangement works well and we lined the new crossing paths with alpine strawberries, 'Baron Solemacher'.

The common fennel is a lovely plant among the tawny autumn flowers. Just behind it a hardy chrysanthemum 'Bronze Elegance' will later be joined by a deep red chrysanthemum 'Apollo'.

Borage officinalis

PINBOARD

Inspirations for the Gooseberry Garden

1 Hedges and parterres in the Garden of Love at Villandry in France

2 Pot marigold borders at Chilcombe in Dorset

3 An illustration of *Borago officinalis* (borage) from William Woodville's *Medical Botany*, published in 1794

4 An illustration of *Tulipa whittallii* by Stella Ross-Craig from *Curtis's Botanical Magazine*, 1943

5 An illustration of a gooseberry by William Hooker (1785–1865)

6 Ornamental cabbages and chard in the Potager at Villandry in France

7 The author's old herb garden at St Mary's Farmhouse in Berkshire

8 The lavender path with standard gooseberries at Barnsley House in Gloucestershire

THE ARBOUR SEAT
The arbour seat was made from thick larch poles, which are now covered in roses and the strawberry vine. To create the corner seat, green oak planks were used because they are cheaper than seasoned timber.

GOOSEBERRY TREE
Standard gooseberries grown on a trunk are much easier to pick than bushes. They can be grown from cuttings in about three years. They always need staking. Broom handles make a good support.

TULIPS

'Generaal de Wet' is an old variety of early scented tulip which is not often planted. The soft orange flowers above the golden marjoram are one of the delights of spring.

AUTUMN COLOUR

The leaves of the gooseberry turn copper coloured in autumn. Behind the pot marigolds, Coreopsis 'Moonbeam' flowers with determined stamina and does not need daily deadheadings as the marigolds do.

ABOVE AND BELOW: *The 'arbour' is the most basic of structures. Made of larch poles sunk in concrete it provides support for climbers. Invisible wires nailed from post to post help the roses and vines on their way.*

The four beds now needed something tall in each one. I thought about bushes of currant, but they would have been too big; or fennel, but that would have turned the place into a herb garden. Herb gardens are a lot of work and not all that useful. We had one in our last garden which boasted woad and soapwort and sweet cicely that seeded itself everywhere, but I never liked it much and it was increasingly taken over by roses, pinks and pansies. We also had standard gooseberries where we were before. Lazy pickers enjoy these, because on conventional bushes the best gooseberries tend to hang below prickly branches often in the mud. On standards they grow at just below shoulder level so you hardly need to stoop at all. Lollipop standards of roses can be cloying, perhaps because their flowers are often too big for the bushes that they adorn. But no one could say that a gooseberry was too big on its little mop-headed tree. So gooseberries went in and at their feet the essential herbs: parsley, sorrel (the French round-leaved sort), tarragon and yellow marjoram. A bay tree was planted against the sunny wall where a peach, a myrtle and a fig also competed for space. The odd rose of palest yellow I thought could be allowed, and as many nasturtiums, pot marigolds (the simple orange ones) and blue borage as I could grow.

The annuals were quite a feature in the first summer. They started out as a form of protest against the colour-free zones that many of my clients seem to want. White gardens and palest pastel shades have been much in demand lately. 'No orange, and I don't really like red' are regular announcements at a first meeting with a new client. But colour is lovely, and blue and orange I find irresistible. The orange makes the blue bluer, as any artist knows. In a painter's garden that I admire, the same sort of colours are used, backed, I seem to remember, by purple. In the second summer here the annuals were boosted with some perennials and I chose not purple but blood red and sulphur yellow to add to the blue and orange. The perennial wallflower 'Bloody Warrior' and *Potentilla* 'Monsieur Rouillard' were obvious choices, and a pale yellow evening primrose was encouraged to seed everywhere. Some blue irises, 'Jane Phillips', were admitted as much for their leaves as their flowers, and rust-red crown imperials, with the tulip 'Aladdin' to extend the flowering season. The borage continues to be an indispensable part of the picture but it is difficult to manage, because it gets too big and falls over, so *Salvia patens* for late summer may turn out to be a more reliable source of blue.

That first summer, while the beds to the right of the kitchen garden entrance were filling with colour, the area to the left, where the oil tank still cowered, was a constant reproach. Three cherries in pots to line the path and continue the fruit theme had been a first thought, but it became increasingly clear that this space would be much better as a mirror-planting of the now enviably pretty right side. The oil tank was pronounced rusty and leaking by a sympathetic plumber, who volunteered that a new tank positioned behind the wall in the corner of the kitchen garden would be easy to fill over the wall from the road and, of course, out of sight. I have to admit that this was not a cheap exercise. A small second-hand car, but quite a modest one, with a high mileage, could have been purchased for the sum of money that was needed to carry out 'operation oil tank'. The beastly thing was taken away by a local farmer who wanted to make it the cynosure of some field, but we were left with its foundations. These proved impossible or too

expensive to shift. Nothing is really impossible if you can afford the manpower to move mountains of concrete, but the budget-holder was not enthusiastic to release more money. With the tank moved, there was now room to repeat the gooseberry garden layout that was becoming such an enjoyable feature over the way.

In the corner, however, a triangle of concrete remained, and the walls, far from meeting at right angles, had quite a curious relationship. Sometimes this is a blessing. Too much formality – right-angled corners and perfect squares – can have a fascist look and the quirkiness suited the relaxed atmosphere that prevails here. There was, too, the problem of getting out past the mulberry. Should the path now end in a round bed around the tree or should it be square like the garden? We tried round. The box plants were set in a circle round the tree and then put out in a square. The square looked right and stayed. Around the mulberry the box plants were doubled in width to make a full stop at the end of the path. I have seen trees set into solid surrounds of box which is allowed to grow right up to the tree trunk. It looks smart and rather foreign in town

gardens, but leaving a gap between hedge and tree allows for a planting of tulips. In the end I may fill it in, but for the time being I like the softening of the formality. Behind the tree, where the path turns back to the orchard, there was room for a group of Venetian-red Cowichan primulas to be planted under the apricot-coloured currant *Ribes* x *gordonianum*. With a *Euphorbia griffithii* 'Fireglow' and some lovage, they make an exciting spring picture. This might look too arty in full view; out of sight the unusual colours seem less contrived.

By this time it was clear what to do with 'concrete corner'. It should be a sitting place for surveying the colours that clients never want and it should have a roof of roses. Not so much an arbour as a bower. There should be no iron hoops nor Jekyll pergolas but a semi-circle of simple larch posts, with some laid sloping to the top of the wall to support the roses. Skinned larch is very basic, but I had seen it used for a vine shelter in another garden, where it looked unaffected and strong. It is also very cheap. The life of wooden posts set into the ground is not long. In time they rot at the base and have to be replaced, but they should last for a decade or more. The rose 'Albéric Barbier' was already growing on the wall, not quite in the right direction but huge helpings of manure and some redirectional pruning got it to cover half the bower in one summer. Another rose, 'Félicité Perpétue', a strawberry vine and a white clematis were planted at the feet of the other posts not in 'Albéric's' grasp. Green oak in wide planks was fixed across the corner in a huge triangle, 3 metres across at the widest place. There two can sit comfortably and a lone reader can enjoy a book with feet curled up on the boards. It could have cushions and I suppose one day I might keep some there, but long sits are not yet a feature of outdoor life here. That left the floor which was concrete rubble or, for the optimistic, the foundations for paving. Rectangles of stone are hard to fit in a semi-circle without much skilled cutting work and they would anyway have been out of keeping with the simple and basic structure.

Locally, because stone is plentiful, traditional paving for yards is with irregular flat stones, or smaller rammed ones. In our garden the paving was free, because it came out of the ground. Gravel would have been an alternative, or a mixture of composition stone with real brick, or small stones rammed into the ground side by side. As it was, we felt we could afford the luxury of one rectangle of stone to set in front of the seat and to have it carved by a friend with the initials of everyone in the family. 'Concrete corner' had become 'Calm Down', carved around points of the compass. This soothing anagram used all our initials in the modern version of the inscriptions that used to grace the gardens of our ancestors. If you cannot afford a statue of ancient virtue, a motto on the floor is the next best thing.

OPPOSITE: *The blues of the hardy plumbago and* Salvia patens *balance the rust colours of autumn.*

ABOVE: *Borage is an invaluable foil for the yellows of early summer, but in a dry year it is hard to keep it going throughout the season.*

THE DELL

The 'English rooms' tradition • A place to escape •
A pool • Spring and autumn colour • Bulbs

The English tradition of rooms in a garden is always appealing because it provides a chance to lose yourself out of doors. 'Losing yourself' is an expression that people use not so much about a physical as a mental withdrawal. In the modern world, most of us have what the English playwright David Hare called 'dreams of leaving': we want to get away from it all. But sometimes the physical and the mental states can be made to merge. For some, in lonely places, by the sea or on a mountain, cares fall away. For others, listening to music provides a refuge from the world. Shakespeare recommended music to soothe the savage breast, but gardening works just as well and as a method of release it is much less difficult to arrange than music. The total absorption that working

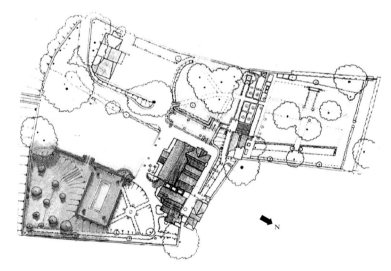

LEFT: *The dell was destined to be a wild corner at the extreme edge of the garden. In the grass, buttercups follow snowdrops and anemones under the new trees and shrubs.*

ABOVE: *Faced with this stony rubble for soil, we might have made a Mediterranean garden, but chose to go native. Box, yew and species roses soon settled into these unpromising quarters.*

BELOW: *The new pool waits for its dark brown liner, surrounded by the yews that spent their first year in the kitchen garden.*

outside demands, as well as the fresh air and exercise, are useful sedatives for stressed lives, but for the deep calm that comes from being alone in a beautiful place, a secret corner is needed.

In our new garden in the beautiful valley, it looked as though escape to a hidden area was going to be hard to provide. From the steep hill under the wood opposite, people on a footpath overlooked our comings and goings. Sometimes they sat down to picnic, and even when they were not around their presence – sometimes on mountain bikes – seemed imminent. Behind the kitchen garden, up by the church, ran another footpath and as the church of exceptional beauty was visited regularly, the sound of voices, of bicycles being propped against the hedge, and the sight of people stopping to look over the garden gate often disturbed the 'dreams of leaving'. Below the church and in the bottom of the valley our delightful neighbours played family tennis on a grass court by the stream. Cries of lost balls and missed shots drifted over the low wall and the gaps in the toothy hedge that grew along the wall all too easily allowed glimpses of the game.

A place to walk and work in the garden, which felt completely cut off from the world, was needed. Below the blue swimming pool built by our predecessors was an area of scrubby grass sloping down to the road. In the grass, some plants of beech and Rugosa roses, with the odd patch of hypericum, struggled to grow. The wall that

retained the slope was low on our side, but on the far side there was a drop down to the road. This part of the garden was visible from the hill opposite and, because of the slope of the land, much of it was seen from the 'No Through Road' below. It was, however, the only part of the garden without a strong identity. The kitchen garden, in the lee of the church, was not a place for the Hidcote treatment of enclosed rooms, and it would have been a pity to lose the tiny orchard with the five ancient, unproductive trees. The lawn was to be the sacred space that linked the house and the view, and behind the house a steep and narrow path offered no opportunities for getting lost. The lower garden did not have so much competition from the view of sheep, of the hanging woods and little stream, nor from the presence of the beautiful church. This part of the garden could belong to us. It was to be set aside for flowers, for a pool to swim in (but not a blue one) and for a shady place. There were no trees, but the presence of a large yew on the main lawn above it hung over the south-west corner.

The curved branch of the holly tree will one day frame the door to the viewing platform above the pool. Propped against the tree is a shell mosaic fragment, which came from Daneway, that magical early Cotswold Manor house with Arts and Crafts associations.

PINBOARD

Inspirations for the Pool

1 The author's old swimming
pool at St Mary's Farmhouse in
Berkshire

2 The calm pool garden at
Knightshayes in Devon

3 An opening in the hedge at
Hardwick Hall in Derbyshire

4 The bathing pool at Hidcote
in Gloucestershire, looking
towards the fuchsia garden

5 The same pool, facing the
other way

6 A close-up view of the pool
at Knightshayes in Devon

7 The beech walk at St Mary's
Farmhouse in Berkshire,
leading away from the flowery
kitchen garden

PINBOARD

Inspirations for the Dell

1 Dappled shade under birch trees in summer

2 Crab apples (*Malus* 'Golden Hornet')

3 Snowdrops in the woods at Walsingham Abbey in Norfolk

4 The berries of the spindle tree (*Euonymus europaeus* 'Red Cascade')

5 *Rosa moyesii* 'Geranium' in flower

6 Sheets of *Anemone blanda* at Pinbury Park in Gloucestershire

7 *Rosa moyesii* 'Geranium' with hips

8 Snowdrops at Benington Lordship in Hertfordshire

Picking up stones was a depressing feature of the first two years, but many of those in the picture above were used to extend the steps seen finished in the picture below. Viburnum opulus 'Roseum', the snowball tree, is a lover of limestone. The small tree is the unusual Malus trilobata.

At Hidcote in Gloucestershire, Sissinghurst in Kent and Tintinhull in Somerset, as well as in many other gardens with rooms, the sequence of different spaces draws out the garden, making it seem larger and much more private than it is. Even when the place is crowded it is possible to find yourself alone in a compartment, so that the feeling is of being wrapped and protected by growing things. Consciously, I did not think of this formula when I worked at the plan for the lower garden, but set out to impose a series of long paths through borders around a formal rectangular pool hidden behind yew hedges. The local contractor, who was building terraces to the west of the house, had known the garden for years, before the swimming pool was made. He remembered a path beside the wall that made our eastern boundary, where old bushes of lilac, laurel and philadelphus grew. Their roots had been buried when the pool was excavated and because the pool was in the shadow of the house in the late afternoon, it had been pushed as near to the boundary as possible. The spaces around the rectangle of water were uneven, which I found disturbing, and there was no privacy. Moving the pool through a right angle so that it lay across the garden and shifting it to the south allowed room for a yew enclosure around the pool. It also meant that we could reinstate the old path running down beside the wall to a door at its end, which led into the road below.

The pool is narrower than most. I had intended it to be 9 metres by 3 metres, but was overruled by the family vote, on the grounds that two swimmers could never pass each other in such a narrow space. As one who prefers a solitary dip at dusk, when others are bored of swimming, I would have kept it narrow for the sake of the beautiful proportions. But it was widened a little to allow enough room for two to pass. Lined with a brown plastic liner and topped with heavy second-hand coping slabs, it looks more like a pond than a swimming pool. Four round bushes of box mark an imaginary diagonal line drawn from the corner of the pool to the corner of the yew hedge. At nearby Pinbury Park, in an enclosure of a similar size – a rectangle of 18 metres by 9 metres – there are green walls surrounding grass with four box balls, and that is enough. Here, the water gives the area more life than the peaceful lawn room at Pinbury, but the principle is the same. At Hidcote, where the pool is bigger and fills more of the space, the water acts in the same way as the grass at Pinbury. Our pool has to double as an entertainment zone. It was important to allow enough room for people to lie in the sun or for children to run around and get warm. Without the swimmers and the towels, it returns to its role as a calm green place after the flowery garden next to it.

The old blue pool occupied about a third of the lower garden on a flat site. Below it, rough grass, with the recalcitrant beech bushes and Rugosa roses, sloped down to the road. To make the new pool and the flower garden, another third of the total space had

to be levelled, which meant that from the eastern edges of the pool there was a great drop to the sunken path on the boundary wall. I liked this, because walking up the path from the door at the bottom of the garden provided a view of the church framed on one side by bushes of lilac and laurel and on the other by the steep bank below the yew hedge of the pool. One day this might be turned into a tunnel, with more laurel and philadelphus and perhaps a wild rose and some honeysuckle on the bank, underplanted with ferns, snowdrops and primroses. Below the yew hedge on the southern side we made another bank to replace the gentle slope. This would give us more flat space in the area next to the road. The bank is very steep, but so is the hill with the footpath opposite. In flat country the banking round the pool would have stuck out like a skyscraper among bungalows, but in the Cotswolds hills are a feature of the landscape. For a gardener, the south-facing slope on fast-draining limestone was a bit of a temptation. This was a place made for Mediterranean shrubs and plants. It could have been a riot, but the flowers were destined for the area near the house, above the swimming pool, and a second helping of colour, even after passing through the cool

Growing trees and shrubs in rough grass is difficult because they have to be kept clear of competition. Heavy mulches of manure, bark and sometimes stones helped to keep the moisture level high. Helleborus foetidus and white willowherb have been introduced in the longer grass, each side of the mown path that leads to the steps.

45

ANEMONES

Anemone blanda *in blue shades is beginning to colonize the dell.*

STEPS

After levelling, the steps needed to be extended to reach the new base of the dell.

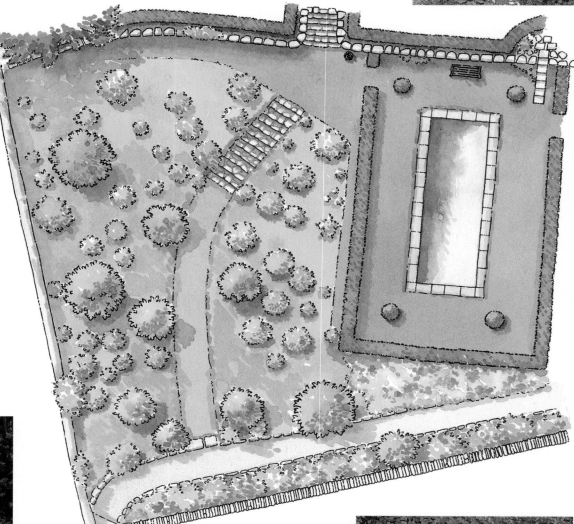

BOX BALLS

The box balls at the four corners of the pool are looking flat on top because they need to fill out at the base before they grow any higher.

SEAT

This seat set into the wall above the dell was buried under ivy and periwinkle but needed only minor repairs.

space of the pool, would, I thought, have been too much. The place where a garden ends and fields or woods begin is always difficult. This was the only area for the trees that would give us shade in summer and protect us from the gaze of others. Although the view of the wood was a dominating backdrop, in the foreground to the south, the roofs of the farm buildings were plainly to be seen. To the east, over the boundary wall that separated us from our neighbours, a yellow conifer and a blue cedar stood shoulder to shoulder, so it was no good pretending that this area belonged completely to the wild. Alien trees like these always suggest the hand of man. The golden cupressus was easier to live with than the cedar. Gold trees look good against stone and in local gardens; clipped balls of golden yew or golden privet are often a feature, planted no doubt to cheer up winter days, when skies match the grey stone everywhere.

Visually, I wanted the dell to belong to the landscape beyond, to the great swathe of woodland that clung to the sides of the valley, and at first I imagined planting a few trees, possibly a group of ilexes, to give us the privacy we lacked. The ilex idea lasted several months. At Cliveden, in Buckinghamshire, a secret grove surrounds a statue of Prince Albert. It is a magical place, a huge area surrounded by silvery trees like giant olives. I planned to grow the ilexes as multistems or large shrubs – as the eighteenth-century landscape gardener Repton did – so that they would not get as big as the Cliveden ones. In our last garden there had been an ilex which we loved and that was another reason for choosing the evergreen oak. The advantage of ilexes was that they would provide a dense screen from the road, the walkers and the alien trees, but although I am often attracted to the idea of simplicity, it seemed sad not to take the chance of growing a few more plants.

In the end, the presence of the beech wood on the hill opposite was the key to preserving some unity in what we came to call the dell. Sticking to one tree, to the ilex solution, would have worked but it would have been dull, and growing anything underneath the mature trees would one day have proved impossible. The beech wood, which I had first seen in October, was a source of wonderful autumn colour. So the idea of a group of trees that would also look good in autumn, as they called across the valley to the beeches on the hill, began to seem appealing. Long ago when I wrote a column in a newspaper, I remember making a ban on attempts at autumn colour in a small space, but I think that I was wrong. Having decided on autumn as a unifying theme for the dell to echo the beauty of the trees on the opposite hill, I began to set up some rules. Autumn colour would be allowed, but in summer the dell would become a green and leafy refuge just like the wood. In spring the beeches are a piercing green and under them wood anemones and bluebells flourish. In places among the beeches, wild cherries, *Prunus*

The pear-shaped hips of Rosa moyesii *are lovely in late summer. Throughout the winter young roses and viburnums need to be guarded from rabbits down here.*

ABOVE: Malus '*Golden Hornet*' *was so weighed down by apples in its infancy that I feared for the life of its young branches.*

BELOW: *The common sweetbriar* Rosa eglanteria *is equally prodigal with its hips.*

avium, and the bird cherry, *P. padus,* are planted, so in our miniature copy-cat wood blossom could also be a spring feature. Pears were a possibility. Perry pears or 'Jargonelle', whose blossom is beautiful, used to be common in Gloucestershire, but their columnar shape is not the best for privacy. Crab apples were a better choice for their shape and for their two seasons of beauty: flowers in spring are followed by fruits in autumn. *Malus trilobata,* with finely cut leaves like a maple, is a delicate tree not often seen in gardens and for years I had been longing to plant it somewhere. *Malus floribunda* and *M. coronaria* 'Charlottae' were old favourites and *M.* x *zumi* 'Golden Hornet' seemed a good idea, because its yellow apples would look as though they belonged to the golden conifer picture over the wall.

If blossom were to be a feature then a few cherries with their spreading branches were also worth considering. 'Taihaku', the great white cherry, has always been a favourite of mine, so that was ordered, although I was aware that it might look too cultivated against the natural wood. It did. Its bronzy leaves in spring and huge clots of white blossom in May looked like an overdressed film star among a group of children dressed in white. In a town or an enclosed garden where they do not have to compete with the gentle background of an English spring, flowering cherries can be lovely, although their presence in summer is never as graceful as the malus. Reluctantly, we removed 'Taihaku' after a year and replaced it with the double form of the native cherry that was growing in the wood opposite. Planted on the bank below the pool this tree would always be seen from other parts of the garden against the wood and it was important that it should not jar. Against the roofs of the farm buildings *Prunus* 'Shirotae' and *P.* 'Shogetsu' were chosen. Their shapes are very un-English, but in that position it was easier to condone them. The shrubs that went in were the yellow-berried viburnum, various forms of spindle berry, including the wild form which grows in the hedges around, and plenty of box and yew plants for evergreen cover, especially against the road and to break the straight line of yew under the pool. Lilac and philadelphus, which we had found growing along the boundary wall, were also used and I chose species roses for their berries rather than their flowers, like *Rosa webbiana, R. moyesii, R. pimpinellifolia* 'Grandiflora' and *R.* 'Dupontii'. But the Rugosa rose which has butter-yellow autumn leaves and tomato-shaped fruit was rejected. It is a lovely thing but would, I thought, have seemed too cultivated for the sort of effect that I was trying to make. In a way, I know the Japanese cherries are wrong, but they are so lovely in the spring that I think they will have to stay. Two *P. padus* were added to the planting in the second year, so that a total of eleven trees was now growing in an area which measures about 20 metres square including the banks.

The flat ground at the bottom is perhaps half of this measurement. In time some trees may have to come out, but the aim is to make them create a totally shaded area so that the grass is starved of light and the ground can be colonized with shade-loving plants. *Helleborus foetidus* (the green native hellebore), masses of snowdrops, sweet woodruff, *Smyrnium perfoliatum*, ferns, lilies-of-the-valley and hepaticas will one day grow under the trees. On the south-facing bank, which is lightly shaded in summer, *Anemone blanda* thrives. On sunny days these flowers open wide, so that patches of intense blue appear everywhere. It is tempting to add other bulbs and plants that would like the hot limestone slope. Already some sternbergias have gone in near the top and autumn crocuses have also been added. Bulbs of the miniature narcissus 'Hawera', which would have loved the conditions on offer, almost went in until Nell, the invaluable and skilled gardener who comes one day a week, reminded me to stick to our original resolution to concentrate on one effect at a time. The anemones would have had much less impact if diluted by groups of narcissi. The beauty of one thing can be overwhelming and for the ground in the dell this is a policy that I know

is right. First snowdrops appear, mostly the ordinary ones, which are divided as soon as they have finished flowering. Then the anemones with the green-flowered hellebores and a few hepaticas and scillas for more patches of blue under the trees, followed by buttercups, which will gradually disappear as the place gets shadier, but for now are lovely. Dandelions we root out: a boring task but they would take over if they were left. After the buttercups there are roses and species lilacs for a little colour, but not so much that you can see it from afar. Then in autumn the yellow sternbergias should be out, with leaves and berries of the same colour. The blue crocuses in autumn may turn out to be a distraction, but it seems worth waiting to see how they will do. The problem with any garden is what to leave out. There are so many plants to grow that it is sad not to be able to grow them all, but concentrating on only a few plants in conditions that they love is often more rewarding than growing a little of this and some of that. In the dell, which was destined to be a cool resting place, this was particularly important.

As soon as the snow melts on the bank, snowdrops and anemones appear under the young trees. In this sort of weather, tracks left by rabbits can easily be seen. The damage they do to young trees and shrubs in cold weather is heartbreaking, but spraying with Renardine helps to keep them away.

THE KITCHEN GARDEN

Traditional plots and potagers • Resisting temptation •
Paths and hedges • Home-made seats • Out-of-season
interest • Fruit and vertical vegetables •
A hidden strip for familiar flowers

Working kitchen gardens always draw crowds in gardens open to the public, and yet they are rare. In the 1950s, easy-care shrubberies and lawns replaced the vegetables that used to feed the family. Rows of edible crops all grown to perfection have come to imply hours of back-breaking labour. But if you like growing your own food, the labour involved is not as demanding as many people suppose, and a traditional kitchen garden is a treat for the eye as well as the table. The fashionable way to grow vegetables is on a reduced scale, potager-style. Little beds bordered with box are laid out in patterns taken from old books, although few of these were intended to be filled with vegetables, because for centuries most gardens throughout Europe grew vegetables in four square

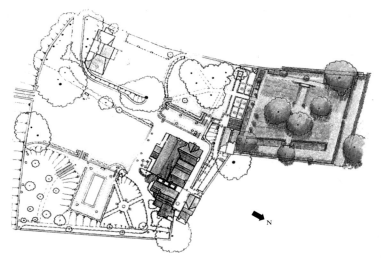

LEFT: *Hostas always attract praise for their bold foliage, but cabbages rarely collect compliments.*
A patch of brassicas, especially if it includes a few dahlias for cutting, is a lovely sight.

A framed view through any gateway is beguiling. Half glimpsed like this, the kitchen garden appears to be a secret enclosure and the sight of the church behind the damson tree never loses its magic.

plots. Success with potagers, where the crops are designed to be seen, depends on rigorous neatness. There is no place in them for the rotting cabbage leaf or the tottering sprout and it is vital to keep a back-up of crops to replace those that have been harvested.

For the luxury of a little untidiness we grow our vegetables in the traditional way in rows. The weeds are minimal, but a seeding lettuce with chicory-blue flowers and a half-dug row of potatoes with the fork to mark the last meal are regular features. I suspect the labour involved in growing vegetables in the old way (which is still seen on allotments) is less than it is with the more intensive potager. In a small town garden I might do things differently, but in the country the simplest way often seems best. In our last garden, we grew vegetables in an enclosed area about 27 metres square surrounded by high brick walls. Up the central path that divided the four plots, arches of pears and roses spanned the way through borders brimming with the sort of flowers that anyone can recognize: irises, roses, peonies, columbines and sweet Williams. These are not difficult to grow and sometimes plantsmen sneered, but the effect was exactly what was intended.

A similar rectangle was available at the new garden, but instead of high brick walls to the north and west, there were hedges of beech and battered lonicera. The stone wall that backed the gooseberry gardens bordered the south side and down the eastern edge a low wall lay under the tower of the ancient small church. A few apple trees, like the ones in the orchard, some grass and the trappings of a chicken-run prevailed, but there was a central path and a couple of stony patches dug out for vegetables on one side. It was one of those places so peaceful and so perfect that the first reaction was to freeze the frame and leave everything as it was, like a scene from *Sleeping Beauty*. Doing too much, adding flowers, bowers, white seats and hard paths is a besetting temptation in any garden, but where fields, woods or buildings deserve attention, less always adds up to more. Hard work and improvement may seem a good thing, but they often end up by producing too rich a mixture for the surroundings. If in doubt about where to go, what 'feeling' to exploit in a particular part of the garden, I think in words not pictures. It helps to sum up what I am trying to do in a mantra of adjectives, which describes the desired effect. 'Ancient', 'peaceful', 'timeless', 'green', 'humble' – these are the words that made a useful formula for the kitchen garden below the tower of the Saxon church.

Most of the trees stayed, because their gnarled trunks contributed to the feeling of ancient peace. The branches were trimmed a little to let in more light on the vegetables below and, in places where the shade was deep, raspberries and currants were planted. The grass was kept on the central path. The width of the path was generous and on either side, where in another garden there might have been flowery borders, we left bands of grass the same width as the path. In summer these strips are not mown as often as the central one, and in spring they have daffodils – not the huge scrambled-egg 'King Alfred' sort, but a humble narcissus that was here when we came. If I were planting the grass with bulbs from scratch I would probably choose any of the Cyclamineus hybrids like 'February Silver', 'Thalia' or the old pheasant's eye narcissus, because they are all gentle blenders into the background rather than 'look-at-me' flowers.

The settled look takes less time to achieve than people fear. In the first summer, the view back to the gate was a reminder of how much there was left to do, but three seasons later the place looks as though it has always been like this.

PINBOARD

Inspirations for the Kitchen Garden

1 Freshly dug and scrubbed potatoes

2 The box domes in the kitchen garden at Heale House in Wiltshire

3 Traditional beanpoles and bamboo at West Dean in Sussex

4 Auricula-eyed sweet Williams (*Dianthus barbatus*)

5 Ripening apples and tomatoes

6 A traditional vegetable garden in France

7 'The Cabbage Patch', a painting by Alfred Glendening (1861–1907)

8 An illustration of the pears 'Souvenir du Congrès' and 'Madame Treyve', taken from *The Gardener's Assistant*, 1871

9 Yellow flowers of courgettes

SEAKALE POTS

The seakale pots in summer standing near the seakale are about to be covered by the rhubarb leaves which hide the compost heap behind.

PAVING

Traditional irregular paving was put down over this area, above a deep pit filled with stones picked off the garden. This helps to keep the back wall of the schoolroom dry. All the stone was found here and joints were left unpointed.

ERYNGIUMS

The steely blue eryngium was a present from Eddie, the retired gardener. Apparently, it used to grow here when he was in charge, but there was no sign of it when we arrived so he returned some from his own stock.

RASPBERRIES

Autumn raspberries are even more welcome than summer ones, because they come at a time when soft fruit is in short supply. This one is 'Autumn Bliss'.

The presence of the church dominates the kitchen garden. The new box hedge was designed to conceal the bright flower bed from this simple view. The large golden daffodils are gradually disappearing, in favour of smaller, paler varieties.

Around the edges of the garden we made hard paths for easy access to frames and compost heaps in winter and for barrowing loads of manure. Even after all this, from the gateway it still looked green and unchanged but the narrow paths of stones were wide enough for a wheelbarrow around the back of the beds. In the gateway, the grass gets very scuffed in winter and I think where grass paths are subjected to hard wear at bottlenecks there are various options worth trying. Sometimes it is enough to stab the ground with a fork in spring to let in the air, while you try for a few weeks to give the ground a chance to recover. Creep round the edge, jump the bald patch or put down boards for barrows, but avoid walking over the damaged area until the grass is strong again. After very hard winters, returfing of the small worn area is a possibility but would probably cost around the price of three rose bushes for a couple of paces squared.

It was a great temptation to make flower beds on either side of the path like the ones we had in the old garden. Flowers, however, are not peaceful in a view so I compromised by slicing off a quarter section of the garden parallel to the church wall with a box hedge. Behind this a separate summer border was made.

The lonicera hedge that we inherited across the top of the garden was less ancient than scruffy. It was infested with ivy and elder and would always be hard to manage. Whereas lonicera has to be cut four times a year, box can get by with only one trim. The old 2-metre-tall hedge did give us some privacy from the footpath that runs behind it to the church, and the decision to replace it was not easy to take. Along the road, the beech hedge suggested that perhaps we ought to carry on hedging with the same plant, so that the garden would have two stone walls and two beech hedges. Beech grows fast, but it is not as demanding as lonicera to clip: twice a year, winter and summer, will usually keep it tidy. But its leaves are brown all winter and under the stone church it might have looked strange. This is not really beech country. Thorn and hazels are in the hedgerows along the roads and I thought hard about using these timeless native plants. Hazels were particularly tempting because their pruning is minimal and I liked the idea of them bending over the green walk to the church in a gothic arch. But that would have committed us to instant replacement of the hedge on the far side of the walk. This was also lonicera, but in better shape than ours as it had been regularly maintained by the retired gardener who lives in the cottage behind it.

He was delighted at the idea of being deprived of the chore of cutting the hedge, but in the end we all felt that hazels would not provide quite enough privacy. Visitors to the church often stop to comment on what hard work it all looks or ask what is being planted, and in summer the questioners come at the rate of half a dozen an hour. It seems churlish not to respond, but a hedge would restore peace.

Box was the final choice. Its dark green leaves would not look too different from those in the hedge across the way, and it would need less clipping. Box was traditional, and it matched the new dividing hedge that we had planted to separate flowers from vegetables. Advice was taken from a specialist nursery on the best and fastest form for our purposes and they supplied a form of 'Handsworthii', a tall variety which makes a hedge quickly. We used two sorts – not a counsel of perfection, but in this garden the additional texture of a slight variation in leaf seems to work.

The four beds for vegetables, which were mainly laid to grass, were prepared in several different ways. The first plot had been half dug for vegetables, but was still full of couch grass and stones. This one was forked over, planted and weeded. From a spring start, the vegetables just kept their heads above the couch all summer, but weeding was tiresome, especially among the parsnips. The second plot was turned over to potatoes, which are traditional cleaners of poorly cultivated ground. This was easier to manage and almost weed-free by the end of the season. On the third, which was not planted the first summer, we employed a man with a rotovator for a morning in early spring.

These are standard redcurrants under tripods made of bean poles with netting attached. Topped by flower pots, so that the netting does not tear, this arrangement is more decorative than efficient, because the birds always seem to find a way in to the fruit.

Under the runner beans half the potato patch has been cleared to make way for rows of winter salads. In the distance, Eddie the retired gardener's pampas grass looks like the smoke of twin bonfires.

He recommended knocking back the weeds in a bout or two with the machine, followed by poisoning when the weeds had recovered enough to start growing again. But because the ground was poor and because spraying is a beastly job as well as an unfriendly one, we bought a load of mushroom compost which was spread over the minced weeds in a 12-centimetre blanket. The area was then weeded all summer, but even buttercups' roots rise to the surface if the mulch is deep enough, making the task easy. The last patch we left as grass, using it as a site for a bonfire. The following autumn it was hand dug and weeded and then used for potatoes. The stones were worse than the weeds: barrowloads of them were tipped on to the trenches dug for side paths as hardcore, which was later topped with hoggin, which is a mixture of gravel and clay rolled into a firm surface.

Growing vegetables in the traditional way, rather than potager-style in patterns outlined in box, can mean an empty garden for much of the year. Allotments are a delight in summer, but tend to look bleak in winter. In the growing months, rows of vegetables add all the structure and texture that is needed. One of the things that had to be thought about in the new kitchen garden was how to keep it looking interesting throughout the year without compromising the resolve to keep the garden looking peaceful and green. Old-fashioned walled gardens often have borders edged with box and backed with espaliered apples to hide the vegetables from the passer-by. In our last garden, the arches of pears above the flower beds lining the central path were in the same tradition and they did provide a framework for winter.

The church tower, to the east and over the wall, more than made up for lack of interest in the empty plots. Borrowed views are important features in any garden and we were particularly lucky in ours. In old towns, the roofscape, seen perhaps through the branches of a neighbouring magnolia, can be a huge asset. In the country, views out to a distant hill or to a large tree can add something to a place in winter that is overlooked at other times of year. The shapes of trees are beautiful when they are bare and, although the apples that we had inherited seemed to be hopelessly unproductive, their winter skeletons added structure to the dormant kitchen garden.

Seen from the gate in the wall at the entrance, however, all the interesting features seemed to be collected in the middle of the space, or to the right-hand side where the church hung above the wooded valley. The beech hedge along the road was a brown

presence in winter and the eye of the bungalow, where Eddie the retired gardener lived, stared over the hedge, rather less romantically than the church tower. A standard apple, 'Crispin', was planted in the far corner to break the view of the house and a short stretch of espaliered pears put in on the crossing path to stop the eye wandering across the empty earth towards the staring window. Each espalier, when fully grown, stretches to just over 2 metres, so two pears for either side of the path were enough.

Originally, I had planned to close the end of this espalier walk nearest the beech hedge with a seat, housed in a shelter of pear. It would be a lovely place to look at the church. However, the grower of vegetables, who had a hard life in the last garden trying to get to the crops over the flower beds, objected to blocking his route to the compost heap. He pointed out that we had made a hard path parallel to the beech hedge so that the garden could be worked in winter without too many barrows crossing the grass. We compromised by planting another black mulberry on the far side of this utility route, in front of the beech hedge, and I was left with two detached sides and the top of the

Below the netted redcurrants, a border of old garden pinks has been collected in this rabbit-free zone after earlier failures in the lower garden. The roof tiles edging the path were found in the garden.

ABOVE AND BELOW: *These photographs show the building of the 'bus shelters', which will one day be covered in a roof of pears. Once the seats, brick-edged grass path and bamboo cross pieces for training the fruit were in, the arrangement began to settle down.*

proposed pear house. Some old oak boards bought from a reclamation centre were nailed to the larch posts which now formed two sides of a rectangle on either side of the path. Two gothic trefoils, also found in a junk yard, were fitted in to make a peephole at the top of the boarding. Oak planks were set across the inside of what now looked increasingly like a pair of bus shelters. On these it was possible to perch, rather than lounge, for a view of the church, provided you turned your head. Two more pears were planted behind the backs of the bus shelters and these would eventually grow over the top to make a roof. All the posts used were rounded larch and, instead of wires to train the pears, bamboos were used to give the structure more strength until the branches of the fruit trees took over. At the beginning the timber looked raw and none of this work met with universal approval. Jokes about bus shelters became routine. 'Ancient' and 'humble' yes, 'peaceful' yes, but 'timeless' not quite, and 'green' the arrangement would not be until the pears got going.

When you get as far as this with an idea you have to keep going and ask yourself what is wrong, look at pictures for inspiration, try mocking up or visualizing various solutions and think about it for a long time. The answer never comes quickly, it might take a year to decide what to do, but for this sort of design by response there is no formula. Sometimes a disaster cannot be righted and then you admit defeat, take it away or live with it. Working for other people I take fewer risks because there is less time, but in this garden experiments are always worth a try. In the end the problem with the bus shelters appeared to be their shape. A roof would make them much easier to like.

I have thought a lot about the final roof line of the pear house. It could be a tower shape to echo the tower opposite, but that might in the end be too much. I suspect it will end up not as a flat covering of trained pears, but as a low hipped roof, as long as this does not make it look as though the bus shelters are trying to put on classical airs. On summer days co-operative members of the family stand holding bamboos at different angles to see what will look best. There is no hurry. The pears will take a while to reach the top of the posts. Left to myself, I would have blocked the route through to the espalier path; working for a client I would have talked it through before starting the work. Family gardens are made differently and the fact that they evolve slowly with plenty of help from all members gives them a character of their own. The plot nearest to the church at the far end of the garden was allocated to permanent crops like asparagus, artichokes, blackcurrants and raspberries. For these more larch posts were needed to carry the wires that support them. This provided another area where there was some height to relieve the flatness of the vegetable beds. In grander gardens, I have used carved wooden apples and pears, or balls or fir cones, as finials on espalier and fruit-cage posts. For this garden it might have looked too pretentious. But the flat tops of the posts needed to be finished in some way so they were finally cut into points.

Beside the path that leads to the compost heap, six seakale pots covering one of the most delicious vegetables that can be grown also added something else to see in the winter months, as did two old chimney pots and a galvanized barrel over the rhubarb. If I could afford to buy the square hand-lights that have now become so expensive, I would add them to the useful ornaments in the kitchen garden. Traditional barn cloches, which are made of glass, would also be better than the corrugated plastic that is used to shelter

winter vegetables. But it is a windy place where glass is difficult to maintain, so we settle for strong modern versions which can be firmly anchored to the ground.

Over the years we have developed an ornamental system for netting winter crops to protect them from passing pigeons. Black (not green) netting is stretched over sticks which are covered in small inverted terracotta pots. It looks better if the sticks are put in at regular intervals and in straight lines. In summer the same arrangement covers strawberries and anything else that needs temporary protection. Metallic cats' heads, with eyes that catch the light, scarecrows or realistic birds of prey set among the brassicas might appeal more to other gardeners who want to fill the empty winter garden, because traditional or workmanlike objects always help to create an atmosphere where flowers are scarce. An iron footscraper and a Victorian line for setting out vegetables, which were presents from friends, perhaps a galvanized watering-can and sometimes a fork stuck into the ground near the bonfire patch are often left outside. I like the associations with hard work that these objects set up. In a garden they are the

By the third year the pears were starting to fruit. In theory it is better to prevent them from doing this early in life, as there is a danger of young branches breaking, so some of them were thinned.

The four box balls at the crossing of the paths were inspired by those at Heale House. They were planted as good-sized bushes three years before this picture was taken. The roof of the lychgate can be seen behind them.

equivalent of the books and the knitting left on a table that give a house a lived-in feel. They imply that someone has just stepped out of the room, or the garden, and will be back in a moment to carry on with the work. Of course, this can be overdone. Houses where there is a deep litter of newspapers on the floor and unwashed coffee cups on tables are not reassuring; neither are gardens where tools are left lying all over the place with packets of fertilizer spilling on to the path. Because of what they suggest, small things that are useful as well as decorative can give more pleasure than ornaments with no purpose. Here is a place, they say, where work is done and people care, where vegetables are grown to feed a family in an orderly way, as gardeners have done for years. This particular device for furnishing a garden is not suitable for those for whom work outside is a chore and not a pleasure. A new trug and a straw hat left on a garden seat by someone who has never touched a trowel would look suspiciously fake, like Marie Antoinette playing at country life.

The final touch for adding winter structure came from planting four box bushes, which were placed where the grass paths cross. Their position was suggested by the box balls that guard the pond at Heale House, in Wiltshire, where there is a beautiful

traditional kitchen garden. The imaginary square made by the box bushes at Heale –
and now here – suggests a place to pause. Square spaces always do: they naturally form
rooms, safe enclosures for people to linger. One day the bushes will be great domes of
green, like those at Heale. I like, too, the repetition of the lumps of topiary that are such
a feature locally. They punctuate the garden at important places in slightly different
forms. Columns of green, of Irish yew and 'Greenpeace' box, among the flowers: domes
of yew and smaller ones of box around the house, as well as the curious symmetries that
will one day stand on the topiary terrace. All these provide comforting evergreen
presences on winter walks and in summer are a cool foil for the flowers.

The vegetables have never been my province. For years, providing them for the
family has been a weekend hobby for the commuter, who enjoys the meticulous
planning and the labour involved in growing them. Taught by an old countryman, he
sets up bean poles in the traditional way and these, with sweet peas grown on twiggy
pea sticks which are the flower gardener's contribution, give added height in summer.
For the hoeing that does not get done at weekends there is often time in the evening
before the vegetables for supper are picked. Provided it is done often enough, almost
before the weeds emerge, which means once a week or at the most a fortnight, the odd
half hour on a summer evening is not a chore. There are more complaints about picking
than about hoeing. We gave up growing dwarf French beans years ago because they are
such a nuisance to harvest. Choosing varieties like 'Blue Lake', which are grown on
poles, makes life much easier as well as adding more vertical interest to the garden.

The long rectangle cut off from the vegetables by a box hedge and bordered by the
church wall was dedicated to the cottage flowers – peonies, poppies, Michaelmas daisies
and sweet Williams – that we had in our old garden, but no roses. Nor would there be
any smart or exotic flowers – only the sort that everyone can recognize. The area
measures about 27 metres by 5.5 metres. This was divided into a border of just under 3
metres wide, a grass path and another narrow border under the church wall. The garden
here backs on to the old schoolroom, where there are no windows and, due to the slope
of the ground, water used to collect in the corner nearest to the building, making it
damp. Over two winters, a huge pit behind the schoolroom was dug out by any
members of the family who volunteered to help. This was filled with large stones
excavated from the kitchen garden, and in a trench nearest the wall of the building,
some hard shingle (rather than porous limestone) was added. This gave us the
foundation for a paved area for a seat to be placed looking down the border, with a
good view of the church tower over the wall. Crazy paving, which was popular in
gardens between the wars, has gone out of fashion and acquired a bad name, but

OVERLEAF: *Traditional bean
poles are a lovely sight. The
cross braces keep them from
being blown over under the
full weight of the beans.
The Iceland poppies are
grown for picking.*

BELOW: *The rich red dahlias
were an unnamed gift from
a gardening neighbour. This
trial plot for dahlias is shared
with sweet peas, which by
late autumn are usually over.
In winter it becomes a site
for a bonfire.*

ABOVE: *The apple tree at the south east corner is 'Beauty of Bath', which can be recommended only for its age and beauty of form. The fruit is inedible.*

BELOW: *This is the view of the church, seen from the seat behind the apple tree.*

around here farmyards are often paved with large flat irregular pieces of local stone. Cut slabs of paving would have looked out of place in an area that was intended to be very simple, so we used the local stone found lying around in the garden and left it unpointed. In the cracks, grape hyacinths and primroses were planted, in the hopes that they would seed. Violets and wild strawberries found their own way there, as did stray aquilegias from the border. It made a perfect place for a wooden seat which had turned the colour of the trunks of the apple trees. This one had belonged once to my mother-in-law and had naturally aged to a silvery grey, but new seats will age quickly if they are left out in the sun. A clear stain in a silvery colour can also be used on softwoods to tone down their raw state. Behind the seat, on the wall, I planted a climber seen at Snowshill, that best of Cotswold gardens, called *Schisandra rubriflora*. This plant was introduced by Ernest Wilson, who was born in Chipping Campden where a memorial garden to him can be found. Although it should have been barred on grounds of being too strange and exotic, I allowed it for its associations with two Cotswold places. If you make rules, sometimes you can also break them, but I think it would have strained the concept of a simple collection of flowers too much to include more than one rarity. Besides, the schisandra is not a showy plant. It has tiny crimson bells among

green leaves in spring and fruit that looks like cherries in autumn. As the only climber on the wall it imposed a strong unity of purpose, which was what I wanted here.

Near the seat on the church wall we put in a honeysuckle ('Graham Thomas') and under the apple tree which frames the opening to the paved area, a few plants for spring – early violas, the apple green *Helleborus argutifolius* and some bright blue brunnera were planted. Opposite the apple tree, a bush of the old *Viburnum farreri,* in its unimproved form, took the place of a few paving stones. This shrub is more graceful than the hybrid *bodnantense* viburnums, which have bigger flowers. All winter it has small scented blossoms and in summer it gives the seat more privacy from the kitchen garden. Otherwise, the view back up the little path that leads down to the seated area would not be completely hidden by box hedge. Along the back north-facing wall of the garden are narrow beds for lining out spare plants. Some we give away, some we sell on garden open days and others we use in empty spaces. Across the central grass path, this cross axis continues past a brick cold frame, which has windows for a lid, to the

In early summer, ordinary flowers like sweet William, catmint, lupins and delphiniums are repeated down the church flower border to the side of the kitchen garden.

ABOVE: *In the church border a profusion of old favourites is the aim. Shasta daisies, cornflowers and the repeated clumps of catmint and sweet Williams never impress the plant collectors, but their unaffected abundance gives me great pleasure.*

OPPOSITE: *In October, Asters and chrysanthemums come into their own. The presence here of the annual cosmos is a reproach, because some comfrey was heeled in when we moved. Despite frequent poisoning, it persists. Until the comfrey is beaten, annuals must be grown. The narrow border under the wall is waiting for ground elder to go before permanent planting can take its place.*

oil tank. This workmanlike area is fine, but from the wooden seat it is more agreeable to feel cut off, in a place where the church and the flowers dominate the view.

Flower gardening in the twentieth century has become a very self-conscious activity. Clever colour combinations and leaf texture – what my oldest daughter calls 'contrastifolia', that is hostas next to irises, euphorbias and fennel, etcetera – are all the rage. In the church border I wanted to make something which contained all the old-fashioned flowers that I had known and loved all my life, without placing them too carefully. It was to be a nostalgia border, a place for picking summer and autumn flowers, and if there were gaps or clashes it would not matter too much.

Fat cottage peonies in red (the species ones were saved for the summer garden), delphiniums, poppies, anchusa, large white daisies, chrysanthemums, Michaelmas daisies, cornflowers, pansies and violas all went in wherever there was room. Catmint and sweet Williams made clumps at the front of the bed; aquilegias were allowed to seed everywhere. In spring the Michaelmas daisies and chrysanthemums are divided and some are lined out in the nursery beds so that they can be added later in the year if there are gaps. Dahlias are also a late summer feature. A good small white unnamed dahlia and the dark velvet red 'Arabian Night' stay in all year, but we do take cuttings in case they fail. The colours tend to be reds, blues, pinks and whites, but the odd blast of yellow is not banned if I like the flower. Late in the year a quilled hardy chrysanthemum in bright gold provides something to pick after the leaves have fallen from the trees.

In spring there is not much to look at, apart from the clump of early flowers under the apple tree. One year we tried wallflowers in the narrow bed under the wall, but they proved irresistible to rooks and pigeons. The cabbages that they had come to eat were covered with netting, but the wallflowers of the same family, and presumably with a similar taste, were not. Planting tulips is a possibility that I have thought about and rejected. I love them and stuff the rest of the garden with their bulbs (which the mice mostly eat), but under the church I like the green clumps in the border with the pink peony leaves unfurling, because they look so promising. If it were the only place available for growing flowers, I would try to extend the season, but it is refreshing to have somewhere that just looks well tended in spring as it waits for summer to start.

THE ORCHARD

The power of association • Meadow gardening •
Old apple trees and bulbs

There are places in this garden where sometimes not much seems to be happening. After July, the miniature orchard of the few old lichen-covered apple trees becomes a shady corner, where the sun filters in a green light through the branches on to the grass below. People expect much more in a garden today than an 18-metre-square plot of roughly mown grass and five rather unproductive trees. On the east-facing wall at the back of the orchard there is nothing, and reproachful glances from horticulturists imply that, unlike me, they would not have wasted an opportunity for growing *Hydrangea anomala* subsp. *petiolaris*, *Garrya elliptica* or other plants suitable for north- and east-facing walls. Some might have covered the apple tree with climbing roses and clematis,

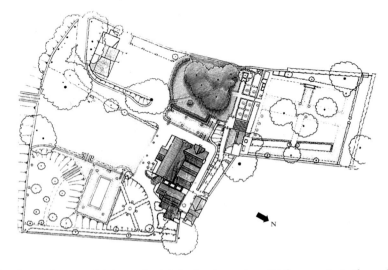

LEFT: *Under the apple trees, daisies and sainfoin dominate the wild flower mix in the early years.*
Any coarse weeds like thistles and docks are hand pulled.

One day the view framed by the apple branches will show only a triangle of green under the wood, but until the yew hedge on the lawn has doubled in size the farm roofs and cars in the lane will continue to be seen.

Sissinghurst-style. Others would have uprooted the old trees and made a formal garden filled with flowers, or have chosen a parterre of intricate box, or an arboretum of different trees and shrubs. But a simple orchard seems to me to be quite enough. The garden has plenty of flowers everywhere else. This is a place that should speak for itself, but I worry that what means so much to me is lost to others. The continuing tradition of the garden as a solace and a place for thought is less apparent today than it ever was.

English landscape gardens have been described as our greatest contribution to art, but they have lost some of their potency in modern times. Those élitist gardens of the educated classes do not speak to gardeners of the twentieth century as they did to those who walked in them over two hundred years ago. The primary aim of a landscape garden in the early eighteenth century was to set up a chain of associations and reflections on poetry, art and the classics. Intellectually, we are impoverished compared with some of our forefathers. We lack the common culture that prompted them to higher thoughts at the sight of a temple, for example, or a group of trees arranged to look like a painting by Claude. But subconsciously, I think, there are some arrangements in a garden that can pull our thoughts and emotions towards common preoccupations. The power of association can be made to work as hard as it did in the eighteenth century, even if the concepts are larger and less specific than they used to be. A response to the suggestion of the human predicament does not depend on the classical education that these gardens of the past demanded. The underlying meaning which gives a place its spiritual resonance is still there for the finding, but I doubt that we would ever extol it in the way that our ancestors did. For that very reason, some may find this line of thought hard to follow. Today we understand sentimentality better than sentiments and nostalgia is rated more highly than the timeless yearnings that we all carry hidden within our beings. A grove of ancient trees is no longer a sacred place for Greeks or Druids but it can still, if we allow it, engender some of the same awe and reverence attached to those tree temples. In the same way, when non-practising Christians go to look at old churches, they are affected by the spirit of the place. Without knowing why they should do so, they talk in whispers or stand in silent thought.

Few gardeners have enough land for groves of ancient oaks, but for fruit trees there is sometimes room. An orchard has not only an echo of the sacred grove, but also a historical association with spirituality. In the seventeenth century, orchards were designated sacred places. A Calvinist, Ralph Austen, even wrote a treatise on fruit trees which included a section on the spiritual use of an orchard. He was not alone in regarding fruit as the ultimate symbol of virtue. 'I gather flowers, my fruits are only flowers,' wrote the poet Andrew Marvell in a metaphysical poem of contrition. We still talk about the fruits of our labours; somewhere perhaps at the back of our minds is a collective memory of hunting and gathering for food to keep us alive, so that the thrill of finding fruit, which, unlike money, does grow on trees, never palls.

Orchards also have another association. For hundreds of years trees have been planted around dwellings to provide shelter from wind and shade from the sun. A clump of trees, as Keith Thomas points out in his study *Man and the Natural World*, has been for centuries a recognized symbol of human habitation. For me, on a private level, orchards have always suggested Samuel Palmer's paintings and in particular the great clots of pear blossom that he painted in a Shoreham garden. If I only had space in a garden for one tree, it would have to be an apple. A proper apple tree, branching from shoulder height above the ground, is a wonderful thing anywhere. The mythical or painterly associations of the orchard or the single apple tree can furnish the space as well as any flowers, but may not be enough for everyone. Our orchard seems to have the best of both worlds: for five months of the year, it is a celebration of spring, with the focus on the flowers; for the other half year it returns to being a mythical orchard.

In spring under leafless trees, small narcissi like 'February Silver' start to grow. Later in the year the old pheasant's eye will produce scented bunches for the house.

APPLE TREE BARK
In winter bark is a miniature landscape, like a relief map of the surface of the moon.

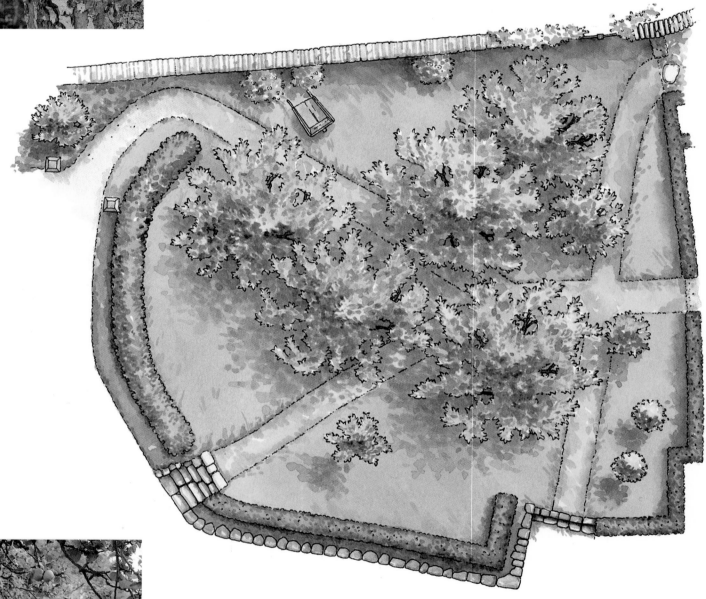

APPLE TREES
The barrow beneath the apple trees has long ceased to move. Ripe fruit on the branches and signs of decay below are reminders of the passage of time.

On our impoverished limestone soil fruit does not thrive unless it is heavily manured, but there are compensations for this lack of abundance. Where soil is poor, wild flowers do well because of the reduced competition from grass. In our old garden, in a newly planted mixed orchard about 18 metres square (not much larger than the one we now have), we had mown paths through longer grass, with bulbs and flowers on either side. Twenty years ago, when wild flower gardening was in its infancy, we made the mistake of sowing a rye grass, a strong grower, under the trees. Oxeye daisies, cowslips, crocuses and native daffodils (*Narcissus pseudonarcissus*) were all planted in this grass, which grew long and untidy in summer.

By the time we took over the garden there was plenty of information on how to sow and manage areas for wild flowers, and specially prepared seed mixtures suitable for different soils with the right sort of grasses were available. Over half of the orchard was already established turf, but the rest, which had been occupied by two long beds filled with Hybrid Tea roses, was raked and sown with a mixture that was suitable for calcareous soils. Both old and new grass were planted with *Crocus tommasinianus* for its early bluey purple flowers and with various forms of wild daffodils, as well as the Cyclamineus hybrid narcissus 'February Silver', which is

In the old orchard the grass was not re-sown, which was a mistake. There is an obvious division between this and the new grass, sown when the terrace was made. But wild flowers from the new patch can be introduced to the old, where after three years orchids began to appear.

very pale and flowers, not as its name suggests, in March. We also put in some large cowslips, the offspring of plants that came originally from France via the old garden. I am ashamed of this plundering now because collecting plants from the wild is no longer acceptable, but years ago on holidays in France or Italy we used to bring back the odd cyclamen corm or a plant like the cowslip to remind us of the places where we had picnicked or walked. In the first summer, a forest of oxeye daisies grew on the newly sown area and in the old grass a few hawkweeds and one or two flowers of ladies' bedstraw appeared, which gave the orchard a rather unbalanced look. It would have been better to have re-sown the whole area with the same mixture, but time and resources were short. There was so much else to do. Some of the daisies and the sainfoin, which is a local flower, were moved as plants into the old grass, in the hope that they would seed themselves, and a few plants of the wild blue cranesbill were raised in the kitchen garden and then transferred to the orchard. Putting small plants into grass is often the easiest way of establishing wild flowers.

There are degrees of commitment to 'wild flower' gardening. What I call the Robinsonian approach, after William Robinson, the late-Victorian gardener who planted peonies and other non-native herbaceous perennials in grass, is lavish and would not have looked quite right in the orchard where mythical associations were to dominate. Introducing tulips and camassias among the buttercups and dandelions, as the Prince of Wales has done so successfully at Highgrove, is expensive and more suitable for parks than orchards. But at Faringdon House, in Oxfordshire, a Botticelli meadow of smaller flowers is an inspiration and an irresistible example. The purist would allow in a wild flower meadow only what grows naturally in the district. I am often governed by that approach, but here the Botticelli model of tiny flowers like jewels in the grass was the one I wanted. I see no conflict between Samuel Palmer and Botticelli but others might, and perhaps in time I may come to regret the richness of the floral tapestry under the apple trees. Fritillaries are not strictly at home in limestone grassland, because they prefer the damp soil of water meadows, but they seem to manage and even increase under the apple trees. Hyacinths that have served a turn indoors in bowls also end their days in the orchard. They spend a year lined out in a spare patch of ground because their dying leaves, after they

have been forced, are not acceptable. Size is what governs the choice of bulbs, for it is better if they appear very close to the ground. If I could get them to grow, species tulips would be lovely, but they have not yet been tried. Primroses and cowslips are divided after flowering and replanted in different areas, but we leave a few to seed themselves. The late-flowering pheasant's eye narcissi are tall but by the time they flower the grass has grown up to them, so they also earn their place. This old form is hard to find and is often replaced with the variety called 'Actaea', but here that would come too early.

In July, after all the flowers have had a chance to seed, the grass is given its first cut. From that moment it is kept cut, but there is always a distinction between the tightly mown paths and the rougher grass where the flowers have grown. A late mow is important so that the grass starts the year short enough for the crocuses to be seen and then lengthens as the flowers grow taller. For almost half the year, from July until the leaves are off the trees, the place reverts to being a simple orchard, with only leafy boughs and apples to provide the interest. For me, that is quite enough.

OPPOSITE: *The orchard is a perfect place for children, where paths through grass must appear as tall as a forest.*

ABOVE: *Oxeye daisies are untidy in late summer but it is important to leave the cutting so that other flowers can seed.*

OVERLEAF: *When the orchard is seen against a backdrop of fields it is easy to understand how a garden cannot compete with the landscape.*

THE TERRACE

*Steps, banks and landings •
Design by elimination • Topiary*

The terrace we made near the west wall of the house was our first project. From the study window, instead of staring into a high wall topped by a bank of heather and hypericum, we now looked up two flights of steps with grass landings, towards the orchard. The view from the window was vastly improved, and seen from the front instead of being shouldered out by a hill, the house was now set in the space that its regular façade needed. But terraces do more than improve the view: they replace banks, which are notoriously difficult to plant and maintain. A terrace creates a level area for gardening. Where the terrace returned to retain the steep ground at the northern end, we made the wall much lower, leaving a high bank, facing south with a stone seat at its

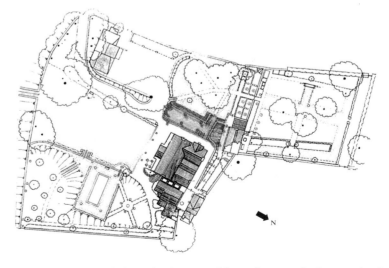

LEFT: *The terrace provided two levels retained by walls, instead of a steep bank
of heather and hypericum that sloped towards the house.*

ABOVE: *At first it seemed irresistible to make flower beds along the length of the terrace.*

BELOW: *Clumps of* Paeonia mlokosewitschii *with tulips 'West Point' and 'White Triumphator' were a feature in the first spring.*

base. It made a good place from which to look down the valley and the bank was a prime site for rosemaries and lavenders to brush against the shoulders of the sitter.

The steps are generous – the width of the window – but their treads at almost 20 centimetres high are slightly too steep. It was a false economy to add the extra couple of centimetres to the normally more acceptable 17-centimetre tread, but at the time the budget was strained and saving the price of an extra step seemed prudent. For the fit, they are not a problem, but for the very old or very young they are less easy than they might be. Going up them on the fastest route to the greenhouse can suggest an assault course rather than a leisurely stroll around the garden. In all there are sixteen steps, if you include the smaller ones which cross the rosemary bank at a right angle to the main axis. The base of the greenhouse is almost level with the first floor of the house, at around 3 metres above the start of the steps. If this had been tackled in an unbroken flight of stairs it might have looked daunting, but the grass path that separates the two flights stops it from looking too imposing. At the top there is another landing where camomile struggles in the stony soil. If this small area is a success it may be worth trying to establish camomile instead of grass on the main terrace. Mowing here is not a popular chore, because the mower has to be hauled up the first flight of steps once a week in summer. A lighter machine might help, but it is a fiddly area to cut and the clippings have to be carried down the steps; in time this needs rethinking.

Unlike designing for other people, making a garden at home can be paced to suit time and money. If the same terrace had been for a place where garden help was limited, as ours is, I would probably have proposed camomile, or paving with a lavish planting between the stones, at the start. But to do either of these would be expensive and the camomile might have proved difficult to establish. At home it can be put on trial and stocks of plants can be built up cheaply. The other advantage of working on the garden at home is that it does not have to be instant. Areas can be reworked over the years depending on how energetic or how rich you feel.

At the start, the terrace seemed an inviting place for *Paeonia mlokosewitschii*, grown from seed and lovingly transported to the Cotswolds. Under the wall that retained the orchard, an east-facing bed was made to receive these peonies and a spring planting of white and yellow lily-flowered tulips. It was to be an experiment in repeated clumps, with first the peonies and tulips all down the length of the border, followed by a procession of *Rosa* 'De Rescht' and *Geranium sanguineum* with honeysuckles on the wall. After that, the clumps became agapanthus and *Salvia sclarea* var. *turkestanica*, in front of *Clematis* 'Etoile Rose' on the wall. It looked all right for a year, with a narrow bed for pinks along the top of the lower wall, but apart from the upstairs dash to the greenhouse we never seemed to go on to the terrace. It was more often seen from above and occasionally from the area in front of the house where we sat in summer. Given the discipline of working for other people, I would have thought more about the purpose of the terrace. Was another border for flowers important? Was there too much work to do? Was it a place for sitting in the evening? What else was wanted in the garden? What would look good with the house? These questions should have been asked first.

In the first summer, repeated clumps of Salvia sclarea *var.* turkestanica *interspersed with hardy agapanthus were tried.*

Inspirations for the Terrace

1 Snow-covered topiary at
Beckley Park in Oxfordshire
2 Topiary in Sapperton
in Gloucestershire
3 Topiary fantasy at Plas
Brondanw in Gwynedd, Wales
4 Pyramids and hedges at
Beckley Park in Oxfordshire
5 Villa La Pietra di Harold
Acton in Florence, Italy
6 Crowded shapes at Levens
Hall in Cumbria
7 Chess pieces at Haseley
Court in Oxfordshire
8 Topiary and statuary at
Beckley Park in Oxfordshire
9 Arts and Crafts topiary in
Sapperton in Gloucestershire

STEPS

The steps were built from stone found in the garden and topped with roof tiles. They are planted with valerian and Erigeron karvinskianus.

TOPIARY

Young yews and box stand apart from one another in the first year but plenty of dried blood makes them grow fast.

TROUGH

The trough on the wall was planted with Iris reticulata *one spring, but later reserved for* Tulipa linifolia *'Bright Gem'.*

Because it was ours, and because I was so thrilled with the space the terrace created, I failed to think properly about the contribution that it was to make to the garden. Besides, the pinks were disappearing as fast as we put out cuttings. The rabbits came every evening in summer to nibble their silvery leaves.

More formality seemed to be the answer. The peony border on one side of the grass was wide and high, and the narrow bed along the lower wall, where the pinks were failing to grow, was no match for it. At one end, the south-facing bank of rosemary and lavender above the stone bench was topped by two yew bushes. When we arrived there had been yew trees wrapped around Douglas firs hiding the front of the small building that long ago housed the tiny village school. The firs were extracted, but their stumps stayed. Removing them from such a steep bank would have damaged the yews as well as the terrain. Left with about 3 metres of yew, we decided to topiarize them. Topiary is a tremendous feature of Cotswold and Arts and Crafts gardens, and in a nearby village there were some wonderful examples. Below the yews, the rosemary bank falls away too steeply to imagine maintaining topiary specimens of great height, but because they are

The yew lumps seen on page 86 in front of the schoolroom soon responded to pruning. By the third summer they had become recognizable topiary shapes. The steep south-facing bank is a prime site for rosemary and lavender.

The view down the valley shows that the terrace belongs to the lawn and the feeling of space that this link creates around the house.

on the bank they look tall anyway. After two summers of cutting they began to look interesting. At the other end of the terrace, a yew arbour to hide the drive had been planted. This was planned to echo the huge bump of yew to the east of the building. One day these green domed caves would stand at each side of the dolls'-house front.

Once I began to look hard at the terrace to see what it was meant to be doing, I realized that the mistake I was making was to try to fit too many ideas into the same space. There were the two different flower beds, the pinks and the peonies. There was the rosemary bank, which I had deliberately kept subdued so as not to compete with the borders; cistus, phlomis and all sorts of Mediterranean treasures had all been resisted for being too varied. Finally, there was the topiary, like a green line drawn at the top and bottom of a page filled with flowers. Topiary was the key.

One of the ideas I had had for the lower garden was to make a collection of odd topiary shapes, out of domes and cones and spirals, a curious village of yew that children could colonize. Levens Hall, in Cumbria, and Beckley Park, in Oxfordshire, are two gardens that specialize in topiary and both of them are irresistible. But the yew village idea went the way of many brainwaves and never came to life. Instead I imagined the odd fat topiary hen, in box, among the flowers in cottage-garden style. We had even brought the beginnings of one from our last house. It sat above the hellebores, refusing to grow a beak. Sometimes we fashioned one out of a metal coat-hanger, but it tended to fall off. Turning the terrace into a topiary walk was much better than settling for a chicken among the flowers. It would be what architects call a statement, something you could not miss. The theme of this part of the garden was no longer in doubt. Four rough-looking cones of yew were planted at the beginning of the garden's third year. The beauty of topiary is that you can take years to make up your mind about the finished article and the shape of these yews is still unresolved.

The flower beds remained a problem. While pairs of the yews stood in the bare beds with the grass path between them, they looked uncomfortable. From above it was clear that for the idea to be really effective they would have to stand in a sea of something that

was all the same. We tried to make the beds formal by imagining matched clumps of agapanthus and geranium down either side of the grass path. We even moved agapanthus and geranium into these positions. There is no substitute for trying something out to see if it will work. All you waste is time. The arrangement still looked unhappy. At Barnsley House, a few miles away, between the Irish yews, random paving stones are smothered in rock roses. It is a lovely idea and one that I considered plagiarizing for several weeks. The feeling that it is only flowers that make a garden dies hard. But the success of the arrangement at Barnsley depends on several factors that were not on offer in our patch of terrace. The Barnsley yews are an axial extension of the house and they have plenty of green space around them, so the fussiness of the crazy paving and the rock roses is offset by the strength of the building and the grass behind the yews. For our topiary terrace to work it had to be grass but there was a flowery consolation prize. The subdued rosemary bank could become more colourful, now that the borders were no longer competing. An arching hugonis rose, more irises and perhaps cistus, as well as plenty of bulbs, might all find places on the hot stony bank beneath and above the green yew forms. The pinks went to the rabbit-free zone in the kitchen garden.

There are plenty of places for flowers in the garden. The terrace is much better kept simple. The yews will become important topiary features in about five years, but as yet their shapes are undecided.

93

THE HELLEBORE BEDS

The view from the sink • Collector's corner •
Snowdrops and hellebores • Copper colours
for summer • Small-scale effects • Improving a path

Plant lovers and collectors always need areas in a garden where the scale shrinks, so that the emphasis is no longer on the whole picture, but on the detail. This is the place to walk slowly, scrutinizing each leaf and petal as you pass, on a daily examination of favourite plants. The border which is designed for long-range impact, the one perhaps that is seen from the windows of the house or from a well-placed seat, needs a bold approach with groups of shapes and colours. The desire to create something that looks good from a distance should help to impose some restraint when shopping for plants. In the places which are to be dedicated to the flowers that the gardener loves best, there is a huge temptation to cram in every treasure that is read about or seen, but, even here,

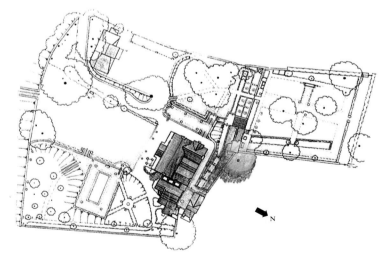

LEFT: *In February cyclamen, hellebores and snowdrops are always a thrill.*
They are near enough to the house to be seen from the kitchen window.

95

In late summer the view from the kitchen sink takes in Dahlia 'Hugh Mather' *and the climbing yellow* Dicentra scandens.

choice is paramount. There are currently over 60,000 plants available to the British gardener. No one can include them all. At garden centres and flower shows, pots of plants in full flower may look tempting, but unless you have seen them growing in the ground it is better to resist them. The more selective the choice in this collector's corner, the more pleasure it provides. The effect to aim for is personal. This can be the place where gardening is as intricate as you want, and where only the best and rarest forms of plants are to be found.

At the back of the house, between it and the boundary wall with the church, is an area of sloping ground, about 5 metres wide. When we inherited it, a narrow flat gravel path lay under a retaining wall that follows the slope of the land; from the back door on the north-east edge to the north-west corner, this wall rises from 30 centimetres to 2 metres. On the retained slope above lay a strip of grass, a path and, under the church wall, a flower bed occupied by a few vines, some peonies and some Michaelmas daisies. From the kitchen window I look out on to this area all year, and the upper path is used daily because it leads to the top of the garden, en route to the vegetables, the compost heap and the greenhouse. This was the obvious place for plants that had to be seen at close range, but it had a rather dank and overcast feeling about it. At the top of the slope stood the schoolroom, beneath the branches of a huge blue cedar planted in the churchyard. Between them they blocked the western sun and, to the south, the bulk of the house stopped the light for most of the day. The highest part of the flower bed came out of the shadow for a few hours after the sun turned the corner of the house and before it disappeared behind the schoolroom and the cedar, but in winter the whole patch behind the house seemed to be dark.

After securing permission from the vicar and church-wardens, the cedar was pruned to lighten its canopy and to lift branches that were rubbing against the roof of the schoolroom, but it was still a shaded area. As many of the flowers that I love best are not sun-worshippers, this was not a problem. The bed seen from the kitchen window would be the perfect place for the collection of hellebores that we had brought with us when we moved. The view from the kitchen sink would be filled with their flowers and under them other winter treasures could be planted so that trips up the garden path would be packed with interest during the cold months.

The grass strip above the retaining wall looked less promising for the cultivation of hellebores than the bed under the church wall, because Cotswold walls that are built to retain banks are always back-filled with stones to strengthen them. If the grass went, the narrow border would be too stony for plants like hellebores that need a rich diet, but I was determined to grow flowers there. The strip of grass would always be difficult to manage, because the mower would have to be taken up two steps to reach it. Cutting grass up to the edge of a retaining wall is no fun and edging both sides of the long, narrow lawn would have been a waste of good gardening time. Besides the practical difficulties, it was a pity to forgo the chance to arrange a walk between two flower beds. Most borders that are designed to be at their showiest from a distance are often disappointing when approached at an angle. They only give of their best if you walk parallel to them looking down their whole length. Double borders are effective, because they draw the walker down the long vista. They prevent the difficult head-on view, because there is never room to stand back and look into the bed. More importantly, for the gardener who is concentrating on plant detail, a second border adds to the richness of the material. Surrounded by flowers, the lingering becomes irresistible; and as you look from one side to another there seems to be so much to see. If the beds were to hold the attention throughout the year, the double border might also help to make the summer flowers look less sparse. With winter as the main focus for planting, the space left for other seasons was bound to be restricted.

The hellebores went into the most prominent positions under the wall. The hybrid *nigercors*, a cross between the Christmas rose and the Corsican hellebore, has waxy flowers and bold leaves and I waited years for it as it was in short supply. The one I really wanted was *H.* x *ericsmithii*, but the queue of names at the nursery before mine was too long.

In late spring the variegated white honesty and green euphorbias dominate the bed. It is hard to protect the seedlings of the biennial honesty from mildew, so a reserve of plants is grown in a cooler place.

Inspirations for the Hellebore Beds

1 Copper colours in the cottage garden in spring at Sissinghurst, Kent

2 Golden holly at Essex House in Avon

3 An illustration of *Helleborus niger* (the Christmas rose) by G.D. Ehret (1708–1770)

4 A box topiary cockerel

5 Flame-coloured leaves of the maple *Acer sieboldianum*

6 Winter planting around the back door of The Old Rectory at Burghfield, Berkshire

7 A mosaic of fallen leaves

8 An illustration of *Helleborus lividus* from the *Botanical Magazine*, 1789.

9 The lacquer-red Japanese maple *Acer palmatum* 'Osakazuki'

10 Topiary birds at Kidlington in Oxfordshire

11 An illustration of hellebores and ranunculus from the *Florilegium* by Johann Walther (1600–1679), published *c.* 1654

CHICKEN TOPIARY

This box hen moved with us. Frequent nipping of the shoots is needed to make the head and tail.

HELLEBORES

Pulmonaria *'Frühlingshimmel'* makes a good companion for a home-grown dark hellebore. The leaves of the hellebore are cut down just as the flowers come into bud to prevent disease.

EDGING DETAIL

Local Daglingworth stones were used for edging. Any large stone will serve the same purpose. Flints are particularly good.

EUPHORBIA

The best large euphorbia is E. characias *subsp.* wulfenii *'Lambrook Gold'. It is an object of beauty all through the year.*

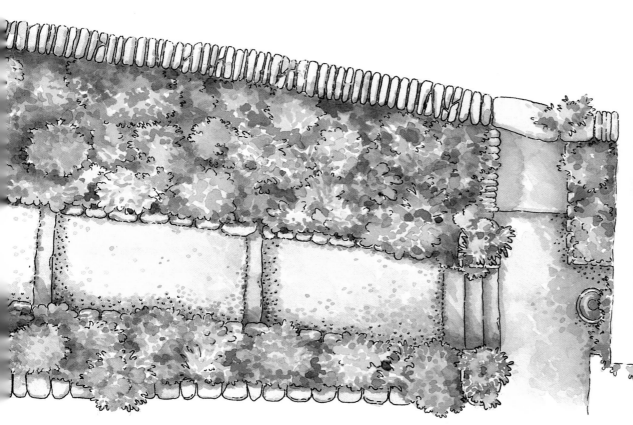

STEPS

Increasing the stone steps from two to four and edging the beds with large stones instead of roof tiles helped to settle the area. New gravel added the finishing touch.

Various named forms of *H. niger*, some flushed with pink and some purest white, were also collected here. The deep black or green or curiously spotted Lenten roses, the *orientalis* hybrids, were to be another feature. Around them a collection of pulmonarias, each introduced after careful consideration, was added during the first two winters. Pale blue 'Frühlingshimmel', and the clear forms of 'Glebe Blue', 'Weetwood Blue' and 'Lewis Palmer' were early choices (so were 'Sissinghurst White' and 'Redstart', a pure coral red). I wanted to concentrate on acquiring the best varieties and decided to ignore all those forms with any hint of two tones in their flower colour. Comparing the merits of each one is an enjoyable pastime on a sunny day in February.

ABOVE: *This is a place where grouping plants provides endless pleasure. Pale yellow primroses are allowed to seed throughout the bed.*

Cyclamen coum was planted outside the kitchen window to make a patch of shocking pink on the coldest of days and *Ribes laurifolium*, with its hanging pendants of lime green, was put in above the retaining wall in the narrower of the two beds. From the path below it makes a more pleasing sight than it does from the upper route. Looking up at the greeny yellow tassels of currant flowers is much prettier than looking down on the matt green leaves. Other plants that benefit from close inspection were also put into the narrow bed on the wall. After I had built up clumps in different parts of the garden, snowdrops with extra special qualities, like 'Galatea', 'Magnet' or the double 'Desdemona', went in. In the Cotswolds, snowdrop fanciers abound, and they were very generous with rare bulbs when we arrived. It would have been risky to put these into the stony bed, because they like deep cool soil, but for the sake of seeing them at close quarters in the winter months I could not resist trying a few there, once I knew they were established in other more congenial homes. A few bushes of white *Daphne mezereum* grown from seed also went in, but when a new neighbour turned out to have a man-sized bush in her garden I regretted not having chosen a better source. Plants with a sentimental provenance are attractive, but in an area dedicated to growing only the best and rarest, associations are less compelling.

Primulas were another subject for collection. The bed produced masses of self-sown wildlings which were not discouraged, and to these were added some doubles like the apricot 'Ken Dearman', some Barnhaven blue strains and 'Wanda' crimsons, as well as various gold-laced forms and the old favourite 'Guinevere'. Any plants that appeared in murky shades of pastel were weeded out.

In summer, as the sun crept over the roof of the house for a couple of hours a day, the larger border turned out to be slightly sunnier than I had expected. During periods of drought, the primulas at the front of the bed sulked. The cure for this seems to be to move them back under the shade of hellebores for the summer. As they have to be divided after flowering anyway, this is not too onerous. In the autumn they move forward into spaces left by summer fillers like *Dahlia* 'Hugh Mather', or the trailing mallow *Malvastrum lateritium*. This semi-bedding-out technique means that I can change the feeling of the bed completely. In winter, the centre of the border where the hellebores, pulmonarias and snowdrops grow is the important area. In summer, the climbers at the back and the plants at the front of the border are the focus of interest.

The back wall is sunnier than the front of the bed, because it escapes the shadow of the house for much of the day in summer, but the north wind that blows through the dry-stone wall does not encourage thoughts of tender southern climbers. Roses seem to manage, although occasionally their shoots come out at odd angles in a bid to escape the cold. 'Albertine', the new 'Summer Wine' and 'Alchymist' all produce flowers in the sunset colours that I currently choose for this bed in summer. Between them, the hardy

ABOVE: *Dark forms of primula are encouraged, but any murky pastel crosses are weeded out of the beds as soon as they appear.*

OPPOSITE BELOW: Euphorbia characias wulfenii *'Lambrook Gold' adorns the stone sinks on either side of the steps.*

abutilon *Abelia* x *grandiflora* 'Francis Mason' and the coral-coloured *Cestrum* 'Newellii' are surviving, but we do take cuttings of all these in case they fail to survive the frosts. Among these I have left room for one passenger, the winter jasmine, which is green from April to October. In the cold months, seen from the kitchen window, it lights up the wall. In the same view, two golden hollies are planted on either side of the path. One day, if the rabbits leave them alone, they will turn into clipped yellow globes. The beds are punctuated by more gold from the cut-leaved form of the golden elder and the best euphorbia, 'Lambrook Gold'. Golden feverfew is allowed to seed itself, and in spring the emerging bright green leaves of hemerocallis add another splash of light. Yellow is often a difficult colour in the garden, but when there is so much grey from the surrounding stone it can be lovely, especially in spring. Forget-me-nots seed themselves everywhere, as does the variegated white honesty, so early in the year this bed, with the last of the pulmonarias, is a combination of sunny yellow and sky blue.

The opening of the big red tree peony flowers marks a change in the colour scheme. We inherited this shrub, a particularly fine form of *Paeonia delavayi* which has bigger flowers than normal, in a sort of crimson tinged with terracotta shot-silk effect. The red and white tulips 'Carnaval de Nice' and white variegated honesty look terrific with it and the golden leaves, but I try to reduce the forget-me-nots around the peony when the first flowers emerge. Gradually the bed turns into a place of copper colours, with less emphasis on the acid yellow of spring and with fewer blues. Now two or three rich apricot dahlias go into the front of the bed and *Euphorbia* x *martinii* with its reddish colouring starts to be noticed as the flowers of the dominating *E. characias* subsp. *wulfenii* start to fade. Plants come and go. This is a place for experiments and new finds; as long as they earn their passage in winter, or come in the sort of summer colours that are in the present scheme, they are encouraged. In time, it may all look quite different. Because the path is in constant use, standards are high. Gardening here is fiddly work and the plants are constantly being fed, watered, propped or dead-headed.

In a dry summer, on our light and stony soil, the hellebores, pulmonarias and white honesty can all suffer, so this is a bed where the new porous hosepipes are laid down in spring and then covered with a heavy mulch. All the hellebores and roses get huge rations of manure in winter, but the hungry ground seems to swallow most of the heap by about midsummer. Because of the retaining wall below, and the nature of the soil, the area is almost like a huge raised bed, with excellent drainage. This means that plants that might not be expected to survive (like phygelius, or the abutilon and abelia) do usually come through the winter, but what suits them is not perfect for everything else. Hellebores prefer a stodgier, damper site so they need extra rations of food and water.

OPPOSITE: *This combination of the dark red tree peony (a* P. delavayi *form) with Tulipa* 'Carnaval de Nice' *was a happy accident.*

ABOVE: *The broken orange tulips worked less well in the same bed.*

ABOVE: *The handsome fern* Polystichum setiferum *and* Euphorbia *'Lambrook Gold' make flowers seems trivial by comparison.*

OPPOSITE: *In summer the copper-coloured dahlia 'Hugh Mather' puts on a bold show at the edge of the broader hellebore bed. The plant on the right is* Ribes laurifolium.

If I were looking for less work, I would probably give up growing them here, but because I love seeing them in the winter months I am prepared for a degree of enslavement.

Quite soon, the plants started to live up to my expectations, but their setting remained somehow disappointing. The path between the beds was so steep that gravel would not stay on it for long. A couple of stone steps at the bottom of the slope and two in the middle helped to break the rise, but coming down was a knee-bracing exercise. When a large piece of stone turned up in a local reclamation centre we had it cut in half to make another couple of steps, evenly spaced between the existing ones. The slope immediately became much friendlier, but the line between bed and gravel was still badly defined. In our last garden, we had used large lumps of flint to edge the kitchen-garden paths. I like this look, which is not too formal, but needed to find a local stone for the job as flints would not be at home in the Cotswolds. There was no need to look further than the pages of the parish magazine, where a farmer was advertising rockery stone for collection in aid of the church. In a corner of a field near the local quarry, I found heaps of the Daglingworth stone that is prized by grotto- and folly-makers. The farmer had thrown it off the fields into a pile and was delighted to have it removed. Arranged along the edges of the flower beds, the stones looked as though they too were growing there, and as the climbers began to cover the walls, the area at last began to look finished and settled.

In this self-contained part of the garden, where we were not dependent on new hedges as a background, it was easy to create a mature look in a couple of years. Well-tended perennials and climbers can achieve tremendous growth in two seasons. As plants began to seed, the problem soon became one of how to find, rather than fill, the space in the two hellebore beds. Now in the third year, I am beginning to wonder whether some of the hellebores might move to better quarters. Flowerbeds that depend on intricate plantsmanship for their effect have to be dynamic. The small-scale interest generated by a collection of special plants is quite different from the peaceful atmosphere in other areas. The change of scale from a busy area packed with plants to one that relies on space and peace for its effect is like the difference between light and shade in a picture. If all of the garden were planted with such intensity it would be exhausting. It is the balance that is important.

THE SUMMER AND WINTER GARDEN

*Choosing a planting style • Seasonal borders •
Nature's treadmill • Squaring the wedge • Differing
levels • Holding the balance • Tender perennials •
Mattocks and stones • Winter plants*

The modern tendency in planting schemes drawn up by designers aims to provide some colour all year round and is planned for minimum maintenance. Professionals adopt this approach because they know that without some degree of skilled commitment to a garden the planting will not last beyond a few months. Often they are right: the people who call in the experts want an easy life and, unless they employ gardeners of a high calibre, the scheme is unlikely to survive. The best that those with a lack of commitment to maintenance can expect is a serviceable, static layout which usually includes some evergreens, some shrubs with coloured or variegated leaves and a few resolute performers among the perennials. Japanese anemones, acanthus, peonies, hardy

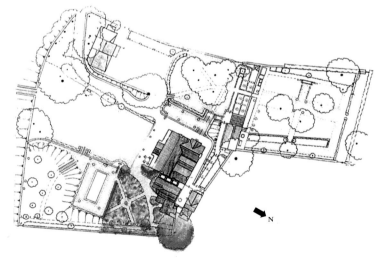

LEFT: *Just before the roses start, cerise pinks of geraniums and acid greens of
angelica and alchemilla need plenty of silver to tone them down.*

109

This was the site for the summer garden. The stones that were not needed for paths and steps had to be wheeled up the slope and down the drive to a skip. The soil was compacted in places, but it was planted eight months after this picture was taken.

geraniums and groups of bulbs might be the sort of plants chosen to provide a few flowers among the unchanging background of leaves. This is a very different approach from the admired planting style exemplified by the artist-gardeners of the Rosemary Verey or Penelope Hobhouse school. In their borders, horticultural skill is paramount. This is what ensures that a changing palette of colours transforms the flower bed, often throughout the year. Without the knowledge and labour needed to keep the show going, this style is hard to copy. For those who want a less demanding task, there are lessons to be learnt from Beth Chatto and the ecological gardeners, who grow plants only where they know they will flourish. Unless Mrs Chatto is in charge, this tactical approach may sacrifice some painterly effects and will probably not last as long as the artist-gardener's display, but it will involve less labour. If, for example, the aim were to grow a silvery *Artemisia* 'Powis Castle' next to a peony or a rose, because the contrast would be artistically pleasing, it would be important to know that the peony and the rose like a rich diet and deep draughts of water in dry summers, but that the artemisia does better in starved Mediterranean conditions. Life becomes easier if you separate plants with different needs, because creating an environment tailored to the specific demands of each plant is hard work.

The artist-gardener approach of abundant flower beds filled with changing colours carefully grouped is the one I like best, but I find that the amount of work needed is too demanding to practise everywhere. In the kitchen borders, where the hellebores grow, I try to keep the horticultural intensity at full stretch. In other densely planted areas, like the church border in the kitchen garden and the patch below and to the east of the house that we call sub-Sissinghurst, I find that concentrating the effect into a shorter season while the leaves are on the trees helps to reduce the work load.

Seasonal borders are often dismissed as being too dull for too many months of the year to be acceptable in small modern gardens, but their advantage is that they do have a high point. The serviceable perma-colour treatment flower beds provided by the professionals never peak, but look much the same all year long. Given some structure to the arrangement, in the form perhaps of a framework of evergreens or a strong design for winter, I like the slow start of a bed that unfurls with green promise in spring and erupts into high colour throughout the summer months. Managing flowers at full blast for a few months at a time adopts an approach that is much more in sympathy with nature's time-scale, as well as being a more realistic undertaking for the gardener.

The serene pace of nature's treadmill is a pleasure because it is so much more restful than our own hurried lives. Gardens that are everywhere at full stretch and full blast give no sense of the progress of the changing seasons. I like being involved in the build-up to the summer crescendo: the anticipation is all part of the excitement. If you go out every day to inspect the same plant as its leaves grow and its buds swell, the day when the flowers finally open is a thrilling one. Sometimes a late frost can ruin a whole year's blooms, as it did in 1995 when wisteria, magnolia and lilac were all browned off just as they were due to perform. At the time, disappointment is bitter but there is always another chance a year on. After such a wait, the flowers, when they finally appear, will be an utter delight. However beautiful the display in a garden open to the public on the day that it looks its best, it can never compare with the plants that you have nursed through infancy to maturity in your own patch. Unless I have witnessed a plant's full life cycle, the finished product for me always leaves something to be desired.

The place which we allocated to our summer garden lies below and to the east of the house in an area about sixteen paces square. The problem was that it was not square, so much as wedge-shaped. I had set my heart on a layout that had been scribbled on the back of an envelope on a visit to the gardens of the Villa Giulia in Rome – a neat arrangement that I had been longing to use in a square garden. The principle of formal

The garden in the first winter. The beds are unequal shapes and sizes, but because the centre is strong, the lack of symmetry ceases to matter. The fastigiate box is Buxus sempervirens *'Greenpeace'.*

beds filled with informal planting is always satisfying. Think of Hidcote, Sissinghurst, Cranborne Manor, in Dorset, or any garden where it is possible to wander between beds bursting with flowers. I wanted to repeat the feeling of these and of our old kitchen garden borders, but this time instead of a linear walk I would create a four square garden. It proved impossible to install. Only one side was straight and that was formed by the new yew hedge that backed the swimming pool. Around the rest, the new path curled down from the back door passing the sheds to go on beside the boundary wall below the pool. I tried for weeks to square the wedge, but failed to make it work. In the

frosts and rains of the days after Christmas 1992 I measured and stringed and staked, until the plot got stupidly small and little flower beds cut out of left-over pieces seemed inevitable. The solution that escaped me for so long was to make a St Andrew's 'X' of paths that meet in the middle. All the beds ended up different shapes and sizes but by placing the large copper container that we had brought from our last garden at the middle of the cross, and reinforcing this arrangement with four columns of evergreen box at the central corners of each bed, it began to look like a garden. Once the centre had been made, the lack of symmetry in the beds no longer mattered. The idea, like all the best ones, was less original than I thought. The Sissinghurst cottage garden, if you look at a plan, is based on a similar

ABOVE: *In the first summer, water-logging was a problem but liberal applications of grit and compost made rapid improvements. The soil structure was beautiful and by the third spring, the beds were beginning to fill.*

OPPOSITE: *Early in the third summer, plants are beginning to look crowded.*

deception. So sub-Sissinghurst it became, and I recommend the trick to anyone who wants to turn an oddly shaped patch of ground into a formal flower garden.

Given plenty of helpers, I might have made the paths grass and the edges of the beds box, but the fiddly mowing and edging of the paths and the hedge trimming involved would have proved too much for our resources. In winter, looking out from the back door, more green would be cheerful and it is sad to forgo the luxury of walking barefoot on grass paths in summer. However, maintaining emerald carpets is a rich man's work and those of us who cannot afford the extra help have to be realistic. The paths became hoggin, without gravel on top, and unedged at the sides. I planned to use plants that would creep over the boundary to soften their hard appearance. Evergreen carpeters like London pride, candytuft (*Iberis sempervirens*), dianthus (if the rabbits would leave them alone), rock roses, thrift and irises were all encouraged to spread along the sides. I also included some summer clumps of alchemilla and hardy geraniums, which have lusher

ABOVE: *Too much hesperis surrounds the dark bearded iris and* Allium hollandicum *'Purple Sensation'.*

OPPOSITE: *'Pink Chiffon' poppies, campanulas and roses in pink and purple shades dominate the beds around midsummer.*

leaves than the dry-looking plants chosen for their winter presence. Moss quickly colonized the paths and this in winter turned a lovely green. In summer some weeding is necessary, either by hand or with very careful applications of contact weedkiller to avoid run-off on to plants near the edge, but this is not irksome.

The best thing about the summer garden was that the site was not flat. From the upper level at the back door and under the arch out from the old yew, it was possible to look down on the plants and the pattern of beds. From the boundary wall path on the eastern side a different view appeared. Here you looked up into the plants that grew 90 centimetres higher than the path. Because the copper blocks the centre, from each end of each diagonal the garden appears different, providing eight different views of double borders. These are short – about six paces long – but the possibilities for surprises are much greater than with a long linear border where the only view is up or down.

With new clients, making a list of their favourite flowers helps to produce a direction for a planting scheme. If, for example, someone suggests lilac, lavender and honeysuckle, it is obvious that they like soft purples and scented flowers. One you have identified a link, going on to think of what will suit the site and work with the chosen colours is easy. When I started to plant I had only the vaguest idea of what I would see at the end, and I began, as I do with clients, by making my own list of summer favourites. For enough impact to bowl over every bystander at midsummer I had to have shrub roses. Green shapes and the favourite verticals, the tall plants that give a garden drama, were also first choices, because I knew that I wanted height immediately to reinforce the feeling of being surrounded by plants. The colours chosen were those that would glow richly against a background of different greens and silvers. Pastel shades were shunned in favour of deep purples, reds and pinks.

When making gardens for other people, the planting has to be instant, so that in the first summer there is something to see, which sometimes means playing safe by using more short- than long-term plants. In my own garden I can choose a process of constant adjustment, until the result is exactly what I want. Perfect satisfaction will never be reached, but travelling hopefully is all part of the fun. Sometimes a planting scheme 'arrives' at a point where you want to freeze the frame, but more often than not I am making notes which say 'Red penstemon looks horrible next to salvia', or 'Try more 'Powis Castle'; less 'André Chaudron'; sack *Lobelia* 'Vedrariensis'.' In the autumn months changes are made, although if it rains hard enough in the summer I try to get away with replanting then and there. Just as I enjoy watching plants while they grow, so I prefer to create a planting scheme that evolves with time. It is all part of seeing garden-making as a process, rather than a product.

**Inspirations for the
Summer and Winter Garden**
1 'July', from *The Twelve
Months of Flowers*, engraved
from drawings by Pieter
Casteels (1684–1749) for
Robert Furber (1674–1756)
as a catalogue for his nursery,
published *c.* 1732.
2 'By the Cottage Door', a
painting by Arthur Claude
Strachan (1865–*c.*1935)
3 The rich and exotic painting
'The Garden of Bey' by John
Frederick Lewis (1805–1876)
4 High summer in the cottage
garden in the painting
'Summertime' by Arthur
Claude Strachan (1865–*c.*1935)
5 Summer borders at Snowshill
Manor in Gloucestershire
6 An illustration of peonies
from *The Ladies' Companion
to the Flower Garden* by Jane
Loudon (1807–1858),
published 1841
7 The deep purples and blues
of iris and anchusa
8 An illustration of aquilegias
from the *Florilegium* by
Johann Walther (1600–1679),
published *c.*1654

TULIPS

The tulips in the copper, out of reach of the mice, survived. Those in the beds were decimated.

GERANIUMS

Geranium psilostemon *flowers a second time after being cut back when the first crop fades.*

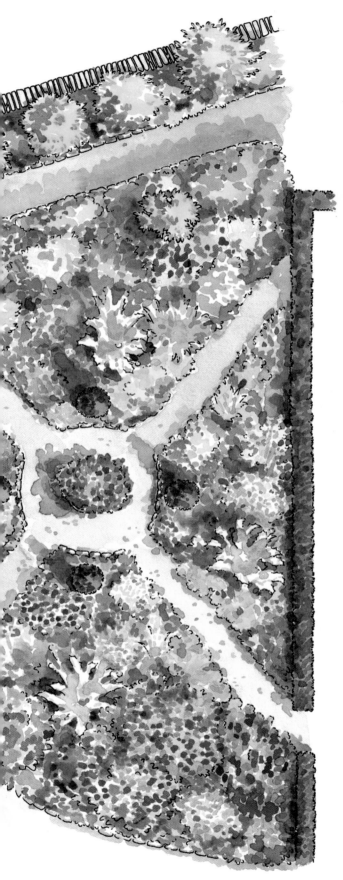

ONOPORDUMS
The biennial onopordums die down in late summer. The gap they leave is filled by the dahlias 'Arabian Night' and 'Bishop of Llandaff'.

VIEW
The view towards the roof tops and the church, with physostegia in the foreground.

The summer garden had to be a place where from June to October anyone on the paths between the beds should feel crowded out by flowers. The ultimate aim was for it to be impossible to look across from one side of the bed to the path on the far side. The largest plants to go in were the trees; two winter-flowering cherries, *Prunus* x *subhirtella* 'Autumnalis Rosea', and the longer-flowering white form were set at each eastern corner beside the boundary path (there were a few concessions to out-of-season flowers). In winter their blossom is seen against the background of holly and laurel. In summer they

The dark purple annual
Malva sylvestris *var.*
mauritiana *appears behind a*
clump of Iris sibirica *leaves.*
The rose 'The Fairy' is just
beginning to come out behind
the self–sown opium poppy.

will ultimately shade the path and a little of the flower beds, so that it is possible to find cool places to stand on a hot day to look at the plants. In high summer, some dappled shade is vital. A big bush of the almost evergreen *Ligustrum quihoui*, the Chinese privet which we had brought from the last garden, also went in on the eastern boundary. To the north was planted a shrubby tree of *Ptelea trifoliata*. Sometimes called the hop tree, it has small green flowers in summer that smell delicious. There is a yellow-leaved form, but I did not choose it because there is so much yellow at the back of the house.

Not all yellows were avoided. I could not forgo the pale sulphur flowers of *Weigela middendorffiana* early in the year on the bank. It is a martyr to late frosts and will probably only flower well one year in three, but I love it. Near the weigela went a *Buddleja* 'Dartmoor' which droops with heavy bishop's-purple flowers in late summer. All the large shrubs and trees are confined to the perimeter of the beds, so that soon the garden will feel more enclosed than it now does.

After the first round of planting, in the second season I added a *Magnolia* x *soulangeana* near the path that leads down from the back door. I will probably never see the garden through the huge Arthur Rackhamesque boughs that it will one day make, but I can imagine what it will be like to walk under a branch that arches over the path while looking down through a green cavern of branches to a sea of flowers beyond. Of course, in time it will change the climate of that bed, but not much, because the tree is planted on the northern edge of the garden above the largest of the spaces.

Smaller shrubs went into the middle areas. Two silver variegated buckthorns (*Rhamnus alaternus* 'Argenteovariegata') and masses of roses. Tall or large bushes like 'Constance Spry', 'Cerise Bouquet', 'William Lobb', *nutkana* 'Plena', *glauca* and 'Complicata' were first choices. Once placed, the framework trees, shrubs and roses were not moved. All structural woody plants start life as insignificant twigs, which upsets the balance of the composition that you are trying to make. In the first summer, roses that should be 2 metres tall are no higher than a bucket, and their flowers seem too big for the bushes on which they stand. The solid blocks of green or grey that will ultimately form the backdrop to the flowers that come and go throughout the summer take three seasons to become a substantial presence. Even the evergreen columns of the fastigiate box 'Greenpeace' were only pencil points at the centre, around the large copper, although they cost a king's ransom to buy as shoulder-high plants. That first year was the summer of my discontent, as I inspected other people's plantings and envied their maturity. The generous gifts of hardy geraniums and alchemilla which galloped across the beds in a couple of months did provide some colour and made the place look full, while more special plants were being raised or acquired. Herbaceous giants and huge annuals also helped, as they always do if you want to make an impact straight away. *Cephalaria gigantea*, the outsize pale yellow scabious, and *Crambe cordifolia*, the

foaming kale, were plants that I wanted anyway. The summer giant silver thistle, *Onopordum acanthium*, has always been a favourite and even when the 'quality' background is fully grown, there will always be a few of these spiky exclamation marks. *Angelica archangelica*, with its green cloudy balls, was another choice for height, as was the dark purple annual mallow *Malva sylvestris* var. *mauritiana*.

'Mme Isaac Pereire' is one of the best Hybrid Perpetual roses. Here it is growing with Nepeta sibirica 'Souvenir d'André Chaudron', the catmint that resembles a salvia and flowers all summer.

The transition from the temporary fillers to the permanent standbys is difficult and as the other plants went in I was aware that many things were not going into permanent quarters. If, for example, the giant thistle is planted near the silver sea buckthorn as an understudy for a few years, it provides more of a contrast to the plants around it than the rhamnus with its creamy variegated leaves will one day do. When the thistle finally goes, more lower silver plants may be needed to lighten the crimsons and purples of the flowers. The shape of the thistle is also more angular than the soft billow of rhamnus. When I put in clumps of *Iris sibirica*, with their pointed leaves like great clumps of grass, I do not really want them next to the thistle, because they look too spiky next to one another, but I do want them near the buckthorn. There the balance of shapes works much better. Ignoring the thistle, they go near their long-term neighbour, the buckthorn, which is not perfect but gives the irises the chance to settle into their final position.

As well as trying to hold the balance between shapes and heights of both the temporary and the permanent plants so that the scheme has a structure, I try to repeat the planting of one-coloured flowers throughout the beds. Plant buffs think this is a waste of good planting space: they will always prefer to grow something different. I like to have a changing background to the rich and rare flowers, so that it does not look too spotty. The perfect year would start with tulips in the colours of boiled sweets coming up between the emerging perennials. They would be followed by clouds of pink and not too much white hesperis, with alliums and aquilegias, then drifts of *Nepeta sibirica* 'Souvenir d'André Chaudron' – the best blue catmint – then campanulas and finally *Verbena bonariensis*. All of these would run about the four beds like the ground colour of a carpet. In theory it works

The ever–present 'André Chaudron' with a penstemon that is always referred to as 'Laura's Red'. The allium seed heads last for months.

perfectly, as many of them are easy spreaders and self-seeders, but because mice eat the tulips, rabbits graze the campanulas, hesperis sows itself where I would prefer it not to be and verbena sometimes packs up in a cold winter, it is harder to manage than it sounds. Self-seeders, like *Lychnis coronaria* and an almost black crimson antirrhinum, are also allowed to be recurring themes. As the summer progresses, the colours of the ground-work background darken, so that the plants they surround also become stronger. If the pink and white hesperis flowered towards the end of the year, I would not want to grow 'Bishop of Llandaff', the dark purple-leaved dahlia with scarlet flowers, in the same bed. With the black mauve flowers of *Verbena bonariensis*, the 'Bishop' and other plants in deep strong colours like *Crocosmia* 'Lucifer', *Penstemon* 'Blackbird', *P.* 'Garnet' and *Buddleja* 'Dartmoor' look terrific.

This is an area where masses of tender and half-hardy plants are grown. Artemisias, salvias, penstemons, verbenas, lobelias, dahlias and occasionally pelargoniums like 'Brunswick' or 'Lord Bute' are all used in changing varieties and combinations. They need to be overwintered under cover, which means taking cuttings in late summer, or keeping stock plants for cuttings to be propagated in spring. It may be that in time this will prove too time-consuming. Or I may take against the rich strong colours and the

exotic flowers and want something that is more traditional and English. It would not be impossible to lighten the colours to rosy pinks and blues with much more white.

More peonies, irises and roses, with hardy geraniums, alchemilla and catmint would be less of a challenge than the present scheme and would be quite happy with the framework of structural plants already chosen, but for the time being I enjoy trying to work with the richer and rarer plants, rather than the more ordinary ones.

To the north of sub-Sissinghurst, a patch of ground lies beside the pump-shed where there is an old well that, until about twenty years ago, used to supply water for the house. The pump still works, but now it shares the building with the filter for the pool. The rectangle of earth next to it is at the north-eastern corner of the garden's boundary. Across part of this ran the footings of a low wall with a concrete capping. For three

ABOVE: *The singing red rose in the foreground is a modern shrub from David Austin called 'L. D. Braithwaite' which helps to lighten the sombre blues and purples.*

OVERLEAF: Perovskia atriplicifolia, Lobelia tupa, Artemisia lactiflora *'Guizhou'* and Hopley's origanum are all late summer features. The rose is *'The Fairy'*.

The winter garden was created two months before this picture was taken. Evergreens and hellebores form the backbone of the planting.

years the area was a dumping-ground for stones dug out from the summer beds. Nettles grew among the piles of stones, and we took to piling garden rubbish at the back of the stone heap, rather than taking it down the path to the bottom of the dell, where another heap of weeds was allowed to accumulate in a corner out of sight. It was the last of the major winter projects. I decided to dissect the space that ran back to the wall under the churchyard lime tree with a path running down to the pink winter-flowering cherry at the corner of the summer bed. In January 1995 our second daughter and best trench-digger started to tackle the job. She had perfected a technique for carving out a trench two spits deep with a mattock and spade in the kitchen garden, so that stones could be buried under a path. Once the heap had been shifted off the new path line, progress was fast, but the concrete topping from the little wall that remained had to be barrowed uphill to the yard. Getting that into a skip is a job for another winter.

By the time the work was done in February we had two large new beds to plant, which would be half shaded by the lime in summer. Some of the remaining stones that could not be fitted into the trench were used to build a low wall at the back of the garden, across the new path. Topped by two large flat stones, this gave us a place to sit on a stone bench under the church wall. In winter it is a suntrap, in summer the lime tree shades it completely. The plan for planting the beds may have been influenced by the season in which the work was done. When the hellebores are out, I always feel that I want to grow many more than there are in the borders outside the kitchen window. I also suspected this patch of ground might ultimately suit them better than their present site. Some particularly tempting forms of *orientalis* hybrids were acquired from Ashwood Nurseries and I decided that the purpose of the corner under the lime would be for winter flowers, to be followed by a green and shady place in summer. We had some redundant bushes of box and a *Ligustrum lucidum* from the terrace borders, which were being dismantled at the same time as the winter garden was being created, and these evergreens were used to furnish the ground first. I had already planted a *Lonicera* x *purpusii* 'Winter Beauty' near the door of the shed the previous year; this moved happily into the bed where its smell could be enjoyed from the seat. On the other side, space was left for a present from a young gardening friend – a *Chimonanthus fragrans* with an impeccable provenance from Christopher Lloyd's garden at Great Dixter in East Sussex. Chimonanthus, or the wintersweet, can be slow to flower, so it is important to choose a reliable source. Hellebores, a new pink pulmonaria called 'Dora Bielefeld', some plants of double yellow primrose and good forms of galanthus all went in, so that by March it looked quite full, but not so full that there would be no room for more choice plants to be added. In the first summer, we planted the ordinary white scented tobacco plant *Nicotiana alata* in the gaps. I would hope that there would always be enough room for a few of these plants.

On the church boundary wall at the back, for more scent in summer, *Lonicera periclymenum* 'Graham Thomas' was planted because this honeysuckle flowers for months on end. For winter on this wall I chose *Chaenomeles speciosa* 'Moerloosei', the japonica which has apple blossom flowers. Near to the path and the summer garden a few flowers for summer were planted. This piece of ground does get sun, so *Gaura lindheimeri* and the long-flowering pink *Geranium sanguineum* var. *striatum* were put in nearest the path. To reinforce the link from the winter to the summer beds, *Buddleja* 'Nanho Purple' went in next to the hedge of syringa on the eastern boundary wall, joining 'Nanho Blue' already planted near the pump-shed door. These airy shrubs are lovely as the summer winds to a close and make it look as though summer and winter gardens flow into one another. A planting trick which Graham Stuart Thomas once taught me is that if you want a natural effect, plants should stray occasionally from rigid groups into one or two outriders, as though they had sown themselves there. The buddlejas belong to the summer scheme, but separating the shady green winter area from the bright summer beds might have seemed artificial. Walking down the path, I hope you are not aware of their differences, since the planting near the edges and the buddlejas should give the illusion that there is no boundary between the summer and winter gardens.

The biennial Salvia sclarea *var.* turkestanica, *a favourite plant, was allowed to stray across from the summer garden into the winter area.*

ON THE WALLS
AND IN THE POTS

*The romance of climbers • The smothered house • Aiming
for unity • A farmhouse pear • The honeysuckle walk •
South walls • Groups of pots • Cornucopia plantings •
The one-plant-one-pot rule • Movable displays*

Roses and honeysuckle round the door are one of the stock images of gardening. Everyone responds to houses where nature clings to the walls in a seemingly artless way. During the Romantic movement, when communing with nature became fashionable, plants began to appear against walls and framing windows. This legacy has never really left us: we are all romantics at heart. Wisteria draped the façade of classical Regency houses; the Victorians liked quaint old houses covered in creepers; and today the tendency is to have walls as vertical flower beds – gardeners cram as many different varieties on to their houses as there is space to manage. Manage is the operative word, since looking after climbers is very time-consuming. They need to be constantly pruned

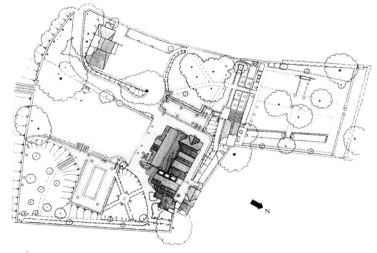

LEFT: *By the front door,* Pelargonium *'Paton's Unique' flowers all summer. Below the big pots, smaller pelargoniums and succulents are collected.*

ABOVE: *The Moroccan broom (*Cytisus battandieri) *fights its way up through the branches of wisteria.*

OPPOSITE ABOVE: Coronilla valentina *subsp.* glauca *'Citrina' flowers all winter.*

OPPOSITE BELOW: *Gold lichen-coloured eccremocarpus colonises the wall that is dedicated to the Banksian rose.*

and trained if they are to look good, and because the footings of walls offer poor pickings for deep roots, they usually have to be fed and watered as well. All climbers can only root in one direction, away from the wall, so compared with other free-standing shrubs of similar output they only stand half a chance. Where there is no shortage of space for growing flowers and the house has a pleasant face, I think there are good reasons for resisting too many climbers. Labour is one of them and ladders, unless you love them, are another.

A better reason perhaps than either of these is that houses of architectural distinction often look better if they are left bare. Symmetrical façades with regularly placed windows can be thrown severely off balance by mismatched climbers. The Regency solution of wisteria-draped fronts with hollyhocks and sometimes a rose below did give buildings a unity that we have lost. The smothered house is here to stay. A dull house can be improved by being plastered with wall plants, if they are carefully arranged and evenly distributed. The least flattering use of climbers is seen when a single outcrop is allowed to spread into a huge stain beside the front door. Less of a welcome than a threat is, for example, the bulk of a ceanothus left unpruned after flowering and allowed to lean out from the wall where it stands – alone. Nor is a single rose, with wooden thorny stems and a dose of blackspot, worth growing for the sake of the few flowers that appear at bedroom-level for three weeks.

On our doll's-house façade we inherited a wisteria across one half of the south face and Virginia creeper on the other. Had I been strong-minded, after we removed the creeper, I would have planted another wisteria – a different form perhaps, with later flowers – and left it at that. Instead I repeated the mistake we made at our last house where there was also a wisteria on one half. The yellow *Rosa banksiae*, with tiny cream yellow rosettes in May, has to have a large south wall to succeed. I am unable to resist it, although I know that in a cold winter it may be killed and that when fully grown it will always be out of control. After the leaves fall, the sinuous branches of the wisteria look beautiful against the stone, but the *R. banksiae* looks untidy for six months of the year. Under the wisteria, which flowers at first-floor level on the more sheltered side of the house, the silver-leafed Moroccan broom *Cytisus battandieri* went in as soon as we arrived. This is a shrub which looks unattractive against red brick, where its bright gold flowers look garish. In front of stone it is lovely. Sharing the same wall, a beautiful tender shrub, *Coronilla valentina* subsp. *glauca* 'Citrina', flowers all winter with pale yellow pea flowers. Through this – and here we start to get crowded – the rose 'Leverkusen' struggles to put out a few flowers and the blue clematis 'Perle d'Azur' is lucky if it can escape the attentions of the mice. They eat the shoots of every clematis in the garden as soon as any green appears. All these share the narrow central width between the windows. Near the porch is a summer jasmine growing up through the trunk of the wisteria and, at the outer edge, *Magnolia* 'Maryland' shares the wall with *Clematis armandii* 'Apple Blossom'. The magnolia will take years to reach the upper windows, so the clematis can have its fling now. I will be sad to see it go, especially as I suspect there will never be room for the magnolia where it is now planted.

On the windier side of the front door progress is slow. I bought a large plant of the *R. banksiae* because I thought it would improve its chances of survival in the first winter, but large plants always grow less rapidly than small ones. In the corner nearest the porch which faces south-west I took a chance on a variegated trachelospermum. It has jasmine-scented flowers and pretty pink and white leaves in winter, but that too is taking time to settle and it will be years before it flowers. The rose 'Guineé', darkest of velvet reds, is also a reluctant starter, but as I want to give it a chance it has to have space. Once it has started to grow I will give it a *Teucrium fruticans* 'Azureum' at its feet. Already a *Clematis florida* 'Sieboldii' is climbing up the wall rather forlornly. It should have the rose for support but 'Guineé' has been left behind. The golden eccremocarpus, always supposed to be tender, is proving much less half-hearted than the roses and the trachelospermum, and that too is wandering about the half-empty wall while the other plants fail to grow. A bush of *Viburnum burkwoodii* 'Park Farm Hybrid' was put on the windy corner of this bed, to act as a filter for the worst of the weather, but until this and the trees in the field beyond have grown up to provide shelter I think planting this side of the house front is going to be a struggle.

Round the corner, on the windowless west wall under the huge chimney gable, I have shown more restraint. This is a place where horticulturists are puzzled by the fact that not only are there no interesting climbers but there is no flower bed. It is a place where ceanothus, solanum, roses and all manner of tender rarities might have flourished, but I have chosen instead to plant one fan-trained pear like the ones I have seen round here on old farmhouses. I do not regret this at all. A little further on, on the same side of the house, there are windows three storeys high on the 1920s Arts and Crafts extension by

Gambier-Parry. Around these, the rose 'Phyllis Bide' and the thrilling pale yellow honeysuckle *Lonicera etrusca* 'Superba' are growing. Through 'Phyllis Bide' a plant of cherry-red eccremocarpus twines. Like the one on the front of the house, it seems to be hardy. It was grown from seed that came from the garden of the painter John Nash, which gives it the added charm of association with one of my favourite artists.

At the back, on the north wall, where the gravel path runs under the kitchen borders, restraint still rules. The reason for not planting too much here is that this, the oldest part of the house, can be seen from the churchyard and I do not want a lavish twentieth-century planting over the wall to break the spell of unchanged peace that surrounds the church. On the chimney-breast there is a golden ivy, which is not performing brilliantly, due I suspect to lack of sun. Outside the kitchen the orange-flowered (but not scented) *Lonicera* x *tellmanniana* climbs the drainpipes to spread over the tops of the small irregularly placed windows on the back of the house. A scented *Lonicera periclymenum* 'Belgica' (Early Dutch) would be a bonus here, but the one I bought with that name is

OPPOSITE: *On the west wall, the chimney breast is for the pear 'Doyenné du Comice'.*

BELOW: *The rose 'Phyllis Bide' and* Lonicera etrusca *'Superba' frame the window. The pots contain* Agapanthus africanus, *a lemon tree and clipped myrtle.*

the later-flowering 'Serotina', planted further down this gravel path. It is lovely but not what I wanted at the time. The only way to be sure of what you are getting when you buy is to see the plant flowering. A neighbour in the next village has a particularly good form of the early-flowering honeysuckle and I am going to ask if I may take some cuttings of that. I plan to add *Lonicera* x *heckrottii* 'Gold Flame' to this area, which has coral-coloured scented flowers at the beginning and end of summer. The north side of the house is perfect for a collection of honeysuckles. They suit the vernacular style of the building and in cool shady conditions they rarely succumb to aphids as they always do in sunny places. It should almost be possible to have one variety in flower throughout the year. I like a quest and look forward to seeing them before introducing them here, which may take some time. For me this adds to the pleasure and suits the budget better.

On the walls of the gooseberry garden (where the theme is fruit and flowers of a traditional sort and only in the chosen colour scheme of blues, oranges and pale yellow) we inherited two roses: 'Paul's Lemon Pillar',

which will stay, and 'Climbing Lady Waterlow', which will go when the fig I have planted needs the space. A very unsuccessful peach, 'Peregrine', has the tips of its shoots regularly pruned by mice in the dry-stone walls. So flagrant are they that when I went up one summer evening to collect some herbs I heard a rasping, tearing noise and looked up to see one half-way up the wall with its head peering out of the stones, eating the leaves of the peach. Furious, I went back to the kitchen and told two members of the family what I had seen and they returned to inspect the damage. We all stood very still and a few moments later, there it was again rasping and tearing at the leaves. So the peach will sulk and the clematis fail until we can face mass and persistent trapping. Serious gardeners in the Cotswolds catch a hundred mice in a winter; others have cats.

The walls are south-facing, but so far a bay tree has not made it through the winter intact, in spite of being shrouded in fleece. For two springs it has sprouted from the base but this never gets it quite strong enough to tackle the winter. The secret with all slightly tender wall shrubs is to buy them as large as you can afford, with some ripened wood if possible. If they can survive the first years, their chances improve with every succeeding season. Sometimes a couple of mild winters does the trick and the plant is away and strong enough to cope if a hard one follows. A bush of the narrow-leaved myrtle (*Myrtus communis* var. *tarentina*) and the lemon verbena (*Aloysia triphylla*) are both given the protection of fleece at the end of the autumn, as I am still not sure of the weather conditions here. We are over 200 metres up, which is risky, but the frost seems to drain quite quickly. In most winters I expect the verbena to get cut to the ground, but it sprouts happily again. All these doubtfully hardy shrubs also have heavy mulches of bark. The rose 'Alister Stella Gray' is quite able to cope with the winter and so is a bush of *Ceanothus* 'Puget Blue' which is now rather out of scale with its neighbours, but is useful for keeping an early white Alpina clematis just out of reach of the mice. 'Albéric Barbier', the almost evergreen rose with creamy flowers, has under a metre of wall space before it turns to climb the wooden arbour in the corner where the walls meet, and through it a vine, *Vitis vinifera* 'Fragola', whose grapes taste of strawberries, threads its way. The other side of the arbour is shared by the rose 'Félicité Perpétue' and a late-

Ceanothus *'Edinburgh'*
on the wall behind the
gooseberry garden is slightly
out of scale with everything
else. Ceanothus are very fast
growers compared with
roses and figs.

flowering Viticella clematis 'Alba Luxurians', which both spread on to the orchard wall until they are stopped by a huge bush of 'Betty Hussey', a new Kiftsgate-type rose.

On the east-facing wall of the yard, where the cars are parked and people do not linger, huge-scale effects are better than detailed ones. I like the rose 'Francis E. Lester' for its apple-blossom flowers and because the late Lanning Roper, who was a sensitive gardener, once recommended it to me. It also pours over the wall by the road in the garden of Nell, the one-day-a-week mainstay helper here, which was another good reason for choosing it. Other old Rambler roses on the yard wall with smaller flowers than 'Francis E. Lester' are 'Adélaïde d'Orléans' and 'Sanders' White Rambler'. On the north-facing wall I have put a 'New Dawn', which has a stiffer habit than I like, but is so dependable with its shell-pink flowers that it had to earn a place somewhere.

Below the house, the south-facing sheds to the left of the path that goes down the side of the summer garden are prime sites for climbers. Their scale is small and I can never find quite enough room for everything I want to grow. Nearest the back door is a fan-trained *Prunus mume* 'Beni-shidori'. This is the Japanese apricot which flowers

In the greenhouse, pelargoniums and half-hardy plants survive the winter months. Pelargonium 'Clorinda' and Salvia elegans 'Scarlet Pineapple' are planted against the wall.

PINBOARD

Inspirations for the Climbers and Pots

1 An illustration of narcissi from the *Florilegium* by Johann Walther (1600–1679), published *c*.1654

2 'The Potting House in St James' Square, Bristol', by Pole, *c*.1806

3 An established pear espalier

4 'Geraniums and Carnations', a painting by Eric Ravilious (1908–1942)

5 Auriculas in terracotta pots, a painting by the contemporary artist John Morley

6 *Wisteria sinensis* on the front of a Georgian house

7 *Rosa banksiae* 'Lutea'

8 A young fan-trained pear tree

The copper in the summer garden changes from year to year. The heliotrope 'Chatsworth' and Pelargonium *'Barbe Bleu' are constants, but* Cosmos *'Versailles Red' has proved too boisterous to be allowed another turn.* Verbena bonariensis *seeds itself everywhere.*

throughout February with bright pink flowers all along its branches. In two years it made 3 metres of growth. Near it is another plant for winter, *Clematis cirrhosa* 'Freckles', which the mice ignore, I suppose because the larder window close by is much more tempting. One of the earliest roses, 'Climbing Pompon de Paris', with pink tiny flowers, is another neighbour. If not watched, it gets early summer mildew. Drenching the roots with water keeps this at bay, although it may not do much good for the foundations of the larder. Round the corner the old bread oven is shared by *Rosa* 'Veilchenblau', with flowers that look as though they have been stained by blackberries, and an inherited *Clematis montana*. This is a poor form and will, I think, have to go, but we kept it for the first few years because removing everything at once makes a place look very bare. A gardening friend persuaded me that Cooper's Burmese rose (*Rosa laevigata* 'Cooperi') was a 'must' for its rarity and I wish I had not succumbed to her horticultural snobbery. For a start, its flowers are white, which never looks good against stone. It is thorny and much too vigorous for the tiny space I have given it. I think I will have it out and give it to someone who has the space and the right background for it, then it can be replaced with the early flowering *Buddleja agathosma* which is already sitting outside the back door in a pot waiting to be planted.

An inventory of all the wall plants in the garden would be long and too dull. There are others that I have not described, and there will be more before what I now write appears in the bookshops. I wish I could be more disciplined about climbers, but like all gardeners I cannot always resist the longing to add just one more. Provided they are well fed and trained it is possible to grow several in quite a small space to provide a succession of flowers, but sometimes I look at the lone pear on the west gable and wonder whether in other places I have not gone too far.

If I have softened up over planting climbers, I remain firm on the resolve to ban flower beds under the west and north walls of the house. One of the reasons for choosing not to make a flower bed under the western face of the building was that when we came that wall inside was always damp. The water from the hill (which we terraced)

collected at the base of the house and the old well-constructed drain, which we found partly shattered under the roots of the Virginia creeper, had ceased to work. The roots had clogged the system and it was no wonder the walls were always wet. With the drain restored and the pear planted, pots now stand along the wall in summer. In winter a large terracotta jar is left unplanted on the corner here, but even then I never find that this area lacks interest without a flower bed.

About pots I feel almost as puritanical as I do about climbers. The fashionable cornucopia style of planting large arrangements so that they brim with carefully chosen plants all grown to perfection can be exciting in the right place, but like grand flower vases they look better in formal surroundings. In smaller gardens I prefer to use pots as a way of presenting plants in isolation. I like to build up groups of complementary plants, each one a single specimen, in the manner of those collections that are found around the doors of Mediterranean houses. There you find geraniums and basil and the odd morning glory growing in whatever comes to hand, which might be a pot or an old

In spring the copper is filled with wallflowers 'Primrose Bedder' and tulips in shades of pink and red. 'Angélique' and 'China Pink' would also be in the beds if the mice had not eaten them.

tin can. These seem to me to be more domestic in scale and to look more loved than the alienating set-piece cornucopia, with a fiercely structural plant at its centre, surrounded by an abundance of the latest in half-hardy plants.

At the centre of the summer garden the large copper is the only container which is planted in what I call the grand cornucopia style, but to break the formality of the frozen look I usually leave a watering-can or a small pot or two of a single geranium standing at its base. At its centre, I prefer to use a francoa, like an outsize London pride, rather than anything with spiky dramatic leaves like a cordyline. Around the francoa are planted the pink daisy *Argyranthemum* 'Vancouver', the heliotropes 'Chatsworth' and 'Princess Marina', as well as ivy-leaved geraniums 'Barbe Bleu', 'Yale' (but not too many of this clear red) or possibly 'Brunswick'. Sometimes a 'Versailles Red' cosmos is added, or anything else that I want to see at eye level and close quarters. The colours are rich like those in the summer garden and the smell from the heliotropes is wonderful. By midsummer the copper does brim and pour with plants in best cornucopia style. The spring display of tulips and wallflowers at the centre of these emerging beds produces the same reaction as a flower arrangement does before a party: it makes the garden look as though the festivities are about to begin.

Outside the front door two large terracotta pots also have wallflowers and tulips in spring, but in summer they are both planted with three plants of *Pelargonium* 'Paton's Unique' and nothing else. At their feet a collection of favourite geraniums and some sempervivums, as well as the odd agave, are grouped, each in a pot of their own. The disadvantage of staging what I call the domestic arrangement, or single plant in a pot, is that many of the containers are small and on hot days have to be watered two or three times. They also need regular turning or they start to be deprived of light on one side. Their leaves have to be picked off and dead flowers removed, but in the cool of a summer evening this is agreeable work.

Throughout the summer, more pots are grouped all round the house on the west and north elevations. Unless you go through the house or over the top and down via the orchard, there is no way of getting to the hellebore beds except by following the lines of the building. The gravel path that we made all the way round the west and north sides runs under the wall of the new terrace, and at the back of the house it lies below the narrower of the

OPPOSITE: In spring the big pots outside the front door are planted with wallflowers 'Primrose Bedder' and the tulips 'West Point'.

BELOW: A close up of smaller pots includes pelargoniums 'Duke of Edinburgh' and 'Mystery', with eucomis and Campanula vidalii.

Around the water butt geraniums in small pots are grouped as soon as the frosts are over. Later in summer they will make up for the disappearance of the variegated honesty seen flowering here.

hellebore beds. Near the pear, the path is wide, almost 3 metres across, and here pots of the tender large *Agapanthus africanus* stand, with a tree of 'Meyer' hardy lemon and a round bush of myrtle. They all spend the winter under glass. Around the water barrel are pots of the intense red but single-flowered pelargonium with dark leaves, 'Friesdorf', or sometimes 'Crystal Palace Gem', because this is a place where I like to see coral or clear reds with no blue in them. Under the only window on this west side a low stone trough has a changing collection of curiosities. *Alstroemeria psittacina*, *Sempervivum* 'Othello' and *Lotus berthelotii* are the sort of plants that make people stop and ask what they are. After the restraint of the single pear, this and the scarlet geraniums make a complete contrast, almost a joke, because they are so bright and odd. Their change in scale is also surprising. On either side of the steps, two smaller troughs have pale orange helianthemums and a range of companions throughout the year. In spring I would like crocuses followed by *Tulipa batalinii* 'Bright Gem' here and in the bigger trough below, but in spite of every precaution, the mice, who like these bulbs even better than I do, have so far eaten all of them each year. Summer is easier. Sometimes the trailing mallow *Malvastrum lateritium*, with pale coral flowers, is added, or *Salvia microphylla* var. *neurepia* and a few nasturtiums 'Empress of India'. It all depends on what we have grown, but clear reds and pinks are always an ingredient.

Further round, at the back of the house, auriculas in pots sit on a three-tiered wire jardinière. There is not enough room for them all, so the less exciting ones, or those that have been duplicated, stand on the ground below. The top tier is reserved for the greenish forms like 'Prague'. Keeping them through the first two winters without a frame has been difficult; cold they can bear but they hate wet roots. A new frame will solve that and allow me to build up a collection of these flowers that I love. All year a winter jasmine lashed to a tripod of willow, and a scented Maddenii rhododendron, underplanted with a maidenhair fern in a copper container, stay outside (although when frost is threatened I do cover the rhododendron with a thick fleece anchored with stones). In a stone trough are tiny primulas and the almost hardy *Begonia sutherlandii*. This shady wall is the perfect place to stand the indoor plants in their resting period. The scented *Jasminum polyanthum*, lilies-of-the-valley that have been forced, pots of streptocarpus before they come into the house, abutilons and a cymbidium spend the summer under the north wall. Sometimes there are arum lilies or the clover-leaved pea *Parochetus africanus,* and some of the plants are tiny, like a species impatiens or a special viola. In groups like these I like the change in scale from large to small. Few of the potted plants flower in the summer, but they do break the line of the wall where stone meets gravel, with a changing pattern of green and terracotta. The beds above provide plenty of flowers. In the yard beyond, the focus of the path at the corner of the house, colour returns. A trough of 'Sweet Mimosa', the clear pink pelargonium, stands under an azara and a cotoneaster. At the back another stone trough has *Fuchsia magellanica* var. *gracilis* 'Tricolor', with pink and grey and white leaves

Auriculas on the wire stand on the north side of the house are a spring treat. They overwinter in a cold frame.

and a few geraniums at its feet. The fuchsias are a whisper rather than a statement as they merge into the background with the green of the door next to them and the grey of the stone. On either side of the steps, where the kitchen borders start, two more small stone sinks have *Euphorbia* 'Lambrook Gold' in each one. Nothing else. Their clouds of greeny gold flowers last for almost six months and when they start to look seedy, the flower heads are removed. The new grey-green leaves are enough to fill the troughs in the months when the sunset-coloured flowers are out.

Some years I have collected groups of geraniums outside the greenhouse, but each year is different and the sites for pots tend to be movable. In the course of the summer they change, depending on how much time there is for arranging and pottering. As I write, I am enjoying less work; there is no doubt that they are easier to manage in smaller groups. In other years I have built up colonies of pelargoniums and fuchsias in the back yard, but if the arrangement of the pots changes, the one-pot-one-plant rule is constant. That is something that I think I will persist with, against the current trend.

ENJOYING THE GARDEN

*Beauty versus grease-bands • Seats and atmosphere •
Choosing routes • Changes of pace • Light and
weather • Managing the place*

When gardeners meet other gardeners they discuss practical things, like grease-bands on fruit trees or how to kill couch grass. The questions that never come up are the ones about beauty. If you talk about gardens as a work of art, there is a risk of resembling Mrs Gurney who wrote verses about being 'nearer God's heart in a garden than anywhere else on earth'. In 1910 'The garden is a lovesome thing God wot' approach was acceptable; now it is not, but it is hard to believe that what attracts so many of us are the joys of grease-bands, weedkillers and lawn mowers. For some, the pursuit of plants is all-absorbing; they are the people who want to discuss the differences between one plant and another. The challenge of growing the tricky and the rare is for them all

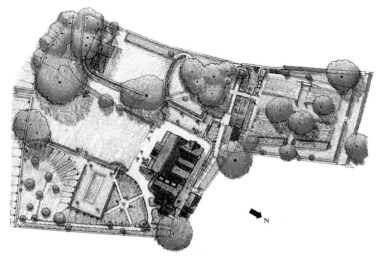

LEFT: *This seat provides an oblique view of the summer garden, which is
filled early in the season with hesperis.*

145

Leaving the dell, the path
next to the laurel, lilac and
philadelphus boundary hedge
that we inherited has a view
of the church.

that matters. Like Mrs Gurney, I would rather talk about what I feel, see and smell in the garden here than what I do or grow. I love a walk at dawn or dusk in summer; counting petals at noon with serious botanists is not for me. The flowers I choose often have associations that remind me of people and places and I enjoy space and shadows out of doors as much as I relish colour. What I remember from garden visits are images, like a table on the grass, roses which droop, a scent in the air, or a green box hedge.

At Greys Court, a National Trust garden in Oxfordshire, by present-day standards the planting is thin. It is a place where there is a tradition of strong simple effects. There is a walled garden where flowering cherry trees meet overhead, a whole bed devoted to peonies, and a wall covered in blue morning glories. This is a garden where there are plenty of seats in peaceful shade. Regular visitors return to unwind after a day's work, and it is that ability to make people relax that seems to me to matter. Those who say that the garden here is peaceful, or that it reminds them of their childhood, have grasped the point of the place. I feel sorry for those who concentrate on the colour schemes, or keep their head down to write the names of plants into notebooks, because in their search for novelty they may be missing something more important.

What I want others to see when they come here is not individual plants, but the best views and the atmosphere of the whole place. This is hard to arrange. Short of guiding people by the elbow, I cannot always make them walk up the path on the eastern boundary wall so that they have the church in their sight line. Often they miss the diagonal glance across the summer garden that we have as we leave the shed. Where we sit above the flowers, in the cave that is made by the yew and holly, there is another oblique view. Unless visitors walk all the way round the base of the house, past the pots and the pear tree, they are never surprised by the view into the little yard at the back. From the yard, looking back, the path is far from tempting. The wall at the corner is high and retains a bank that is so steep and windy that it is given over to comfrey. The path is too pinched around the corner to leave room to plant at the base of the retaining wall. So blank grey stones are all there is to see. One day I may solve this. A stone inscription on the wall would be one answer, and an evergreen that can face total shade and perpetual damp, planted where the path widens and trained back towards the unwelcoming corner, would certainly soften the view. Even a variegated cotoneaster or a pyracantha would be more cheerful than damp stones. When approached from the front, rather than the back of the house, the north-west corner ceases to be a problem, because as it is turned, the surprise of the courtyard is revealed. The one-way system is a lazy solution, but the view to the yard is such a successful and surprising feature that I want to be certain that no one misses it.

Another important stopping place is at the gateway to the kitchen garden. The wall at the back of the gooseberry gardens keeps the vegetables hidden, until the opening where the vegetables and the first close-up of the church appears. When visitors come they often turn left once inside the kitchen garden to carry on uphill towards the compost heap. Do people naturally walk in a clockwise direction? This is something which I suspect but cannot prove. So they continue to head for the compost rather than down the path to the right, which is lined with standard redcurrants on one side and nursery beds under the wall. My preferred path leads to the paved area under the apple tree, where there is a seat. That way, the wanderer arrives at the long view towards the church down the border of simple flowers. If I sit anywhere in the garden it is here.

This business of 'routeing' people, so that they see things the way you want them to be seen or end up at the seats where you want them to sit, is not easy. The mystery of what lies around the corner, or at the end of the path, is what makes a garden feel

This oak gate sets the scene for the kitchen garden. It replaced a thin wrought iron modern version which seemed out of keeping with the view behind.

ABOVE: *The pool makes a quiet change after the flowers in the summer garden. When the yews are grown the entrance will be almost concealed.*

OPPOSITE: *The path on the north side of the house is a standing out area for plants in summer.*

special. But having turned the corner, there ought to be some reward. A change of pace or mood is enough to fulfil the promise, but, for real drama, presentation is everything. The pool garden provides a breathing space, a green pause, after the bright flowers of the summer beds. We had something similar at our last garden, where a corridor of green beech hedge was the cool space after the brightness of the borders in the kitchen garden. That green walk presented a long view to a gate in the field beyond, which made a thrilling contrast to the busy flower-packed place left behind. The green pool room here is nothing like so successful. I suspect that if I had been able to arrange the entrance in the centre of the pool's short side – to give the water added length and to emphasize the formality of the symmetrical layout – it would have been much better. Because of the levels, however, it was impossible to create enough flat space to do this. So although the area provides a change of pace, it lacks the drama that it might have had. With the kitchen garden we were lucky: if the gap in the wall had been set in the corner, that first view would have been totally different. From the corner, across the planted rows of vegetables, the garden looks busy, but at its green centre the mood is calm. After the gooseberry gardens a rest is better than a riot, so the central entry works best.

Sight lines with maximum length are always a bonus but they are hard to create where space is short. Sometimes the best way to do this is to borrow a view to a distant feature beyond the boundary. At forty paces our lawn is not long compared with that of most similar-sized houses, but by opening the view at the end it has been made to seem larger. In doing this, we have lost some privacy: if our neighbours put up a satellite dish in the sight line, a hedge to hide it would be vital, but I would hope that we could still see over it to the fields beyond, rather than sit behind the impenetrable screen that our predecessors made to banish the horizon.

Some views, unlike the one beyond the lawn, cannot be cleared once and for all, so cutting off branches to keep them open is regular summer work. Pruning to reveal views is an art. Russell Page once described pruning a tree as 'working with space, carving the empty air into volumes caught in the angles of branch crossing branch and held by leafy sprays'. Along the eastern boundary path towards the church, the line of vision is sometimes threatened by the winter-flowering cherry. In the orchard the shade under the trees is dappled only if some thinning takes place, and the shape that the branches make is an important feature. Apple trees with open centres and graceful boughs are as lovely unadorned as when they carry blossom or fruit. Elsewhere, screening is more important than clearing. Barrow loads of manure encourage the rhubarb to grow to an enormous size, so that in summer the compost heap is well hidden.

OVERLEAF: *It was impossible to stage the drama of approaching the pool from the centre of the narrow end. The entrance at the top of the long side provides a change of pace, but less contrast than this arrangement.*

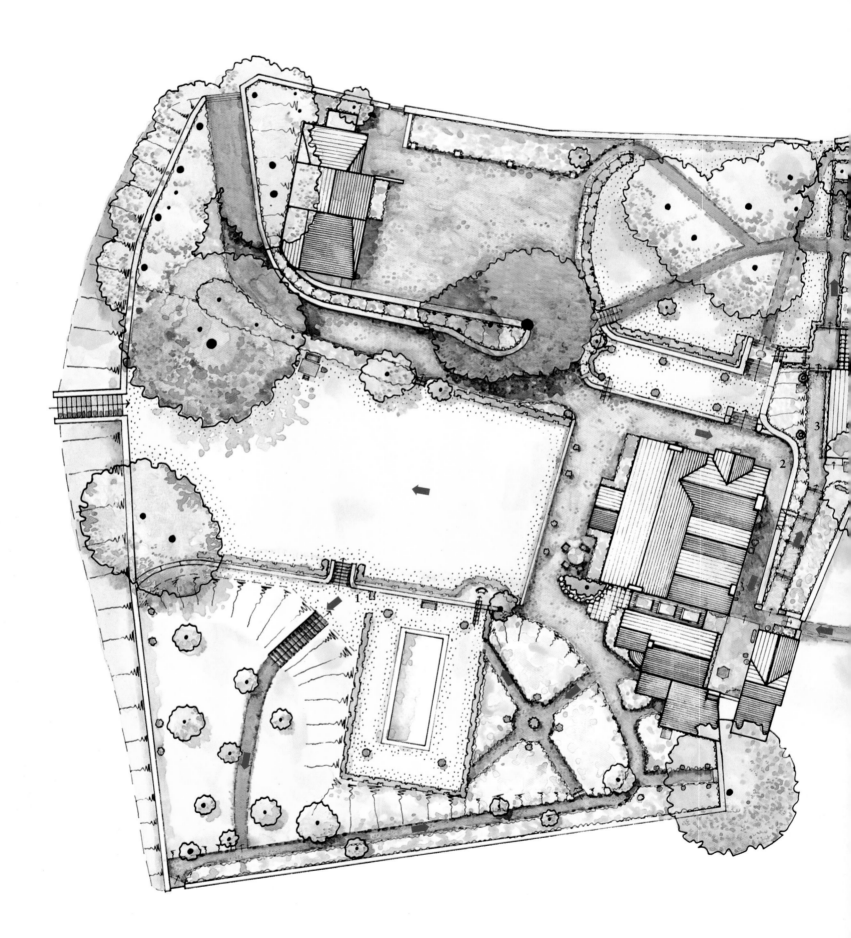

ROUTES AROUND THE GARDEN

The routes through the garden are designed to present the best views and the surprises. There are always times when the routes vary, but it is important to identify the long lines of vision, the vistas that show a place to best advantage.

1 Entering the dell through the stone steps outside the pool garden means that the return journey is taken up the boundary path crowned by a view of the church. Walking down the same path with the church out of sight the entrance to the dell seems more exciting, but the view of the church is lost.

2 The surprise vista from the bleak north-west corner of the house, back to the welcoming yard with pots and a table, is never seen if the path around the west face of the house turns up the steps to the orchard.

3 The topiary terrace is best seen from above and below, and the hellebore beds tend to get missed if the north-west passage is avoided.

4 In the kitchen garden, turning right just beyond the gate ensures the best view of the church borders.

N

| 0 | 5m | 10m |

| 0 | 10ft | 20ft | 30ft |

The philadelphus hedge that grows along the eastern boundary is pruned after it has finished flowering around midsummer, but not so much that unsightly gaps appear.

Working in the garden, we are surprised more often than strangers. Anyone who looks after their own patch knows that there is a different angle on things from every square foot of earth. As you kneel to plant out, or turn aside to throw something in the barrow, new perspectives appear: things are different every day. Light and weather change things too, so that ordinary plants in the early morning or as the sun goes down are touched with magic auras. After rain the whole garden looks rinsed and the earth smells: on hot days the plants are heavy with the weight of summer, but in winter everything stands out sharply. The unpredictability of the special effects of light or weather, or the timing of plants which do not always flower when you want them to, means that the details of planting schemes can easily be lost or blurred. This is why going for a mood or a feeling is easier than trying to organize flowers into a set piece. Planning a garden by concepts, rather than by layouts on paper, is also less work.

The garden here is not maintained to the highest horticultural standards. We have neither the time nor the knowledge to create perfect lawns, nor to grow all the plants as they should be grown. The two of us, who live here all the time, manage the work in the intervals of busy lives – that is at weekends and in odd hours. As well as this, we have two mornings of skilled help a week for most of the year and in summer an extra half day from less skilled, but willing, helpers. A close look will reveal all sorts of deficiencies in maintenance, and there are fewer rare plants than many others grow, but it is part of my philosophy that gardens do not have to be complicated or demanding to fulfil our needs. They should be, as this one is for us, pure pleasure.

The table in the back yard is useful for potting as well as for meals outside. It looks up the hellebore beds to the schoolroom. In the pot is Begonia fuchsioides.

PART TWO:
TRICKS OF THE TRADE

THE DESIGN PROCESS

Anyone can grow things. Gardening is technically easier than looking after a baby or cooking a delicious meal. It is the arrangement, the whole concept of a garden, that is hard. Try to remember that simplicity is the key, which means that for roughly every 7 square metres of land that is owned you should stick to one theme. Everything that is put or planted there should underline that one idea, and the more refined the concept, the better the garden will be. The personality of the owner as well as the house and the immovable elements of the plot will also be an influence. Keep it simple, keep it suitable and leave the plants until the overall concept is decided. And if discovering what it is that you want in the garden seems impossible, then other people's gardens are there for inspiration.

DECIDING WHAT YOU WANT

Looking at gardens, not at individual plants, is the best way of learning to make a garden, provided you ask yourself all the time: do I like it? will it work for me? As you walk around an open garden, try to imagine what it would be like to live there. If there are seats, sit down and think about the atmosphere created around them. If you like the feeling of the place, then analyse what you see. After several visits to different gardens you may find that the notes you take record the same features. If you always respond to romantically grown roses, or to shady bowers, if cottage gardens seem more attractive than the gardens which are collections of rare plants, or the ones which major in paving and architectural features, or the ones which look a bit of a mess, then that is the stage you need to reach before you start to make a plan. Settling what you want is an important step in designing a garden, but the look or the feeling that you decide to recreate at home is only part of the process. The garden that you admire cannot be imposed on, but must be adapted to, your particular site. If it fights too much with what you already have, think again.

Begin indoors. Look out of the windows in the sitting room, the kitchen and at the view that you see first thing in the morning, and write down what you like or hate about it. Can you see traffic, or a tree or the neighbours' washing? Is your plot rank and weedy, or is it just plain dull? Then imagine one or two of the features that you would like to see reproduced from your garden visits and, if you can, draw them on the window glass with a felt tip pen. You might outline shrubs against the boundary wall to hide the neighbour, or the cars, or a flower bed at the end of the garden that you can look at from the house. Keep your dream garden in mind as you do this and choose trees or groups of plants in arrangements that do not conflict with what you are trying to reproduce.

Some gardens are purely for looking at, but the best ones are for being in. Now walk outside and think about what you want the garden to feel like. Is it to be secret, or peaceful, or a riot of flowers, or do you want space and a place to sit? Is it to be formal, with beds in a pattern, or would a flowing layout suit you and the house better? The framed picture of the garden that you saw from inside the house may not fit with how you want the garden to feel when you are outside and walking about. Gardens are moving pictures that change as you cover the ground. Sit down and they change again. Plants that you looked down

OPPOSITE: *Shady places seem beguiling, but choosing to plant these spreading cherry trees would make growing flowers difficult.*

ABOVE: *In this small town garden, the arch hints at more to see beyond, as well as an invitation to sit outside the door.*

upon when standing loom larger from a garden seat. Take a chair with you and try it in lots of places. If the view from the only corner that is out of the wind presents you with a blank wall, a pylon or a hedge of someone else's *leylandii*, think what might improve it. Or move the chair. The designs that you want to impose on the garden from inside and outside are overlaid with the recollection of the dream garden but they will also have to be reconciled to the spirit of the place. Is the house traditional or modern, and what is it made of? Will what you want to see, or be in, look equally good with the brick, stone or paint of the building? Will it clash with the countryside? A purple tree in a green view could turn out to be an eyesore.

THE SITE

Nature also has designs on your design. Unless you are prepared to work phenomenally hard you will have to accept or modify the prevailing conditions. Under dark trees you will never make the cottage garden at Sissinghurst; in a sun-baked plot it will take a bit of time to achieve a cool green retreat. From garden visits you will perhaps have absorbed the fact that roses grow in the sun (although there are exceptions to this rule) and that ferns usually appear in deep shade. Books are a short cut to more information of this kind. The best ones provide lists of plants for sun and shade and will tell you which plants can stand drought and which need plenty of water. The more a plant likes where you put it, the less work it is to keep it there. Beth Chatto is the arch-empress of advice on the right plant for the right place. Those who follow her lead will be growing plants in something approaching their natural habitat. They will find gardening less work than those who want to grow the sort of flowers that you see in late Victorian watercolours of cottage gardens, because these tend to need much feeding, watering, propping and protecting.

In the early stages of planning you need only a rough idea of what you want to grow in the flower beds, so choose one or two key plants and check that these will not be killed by the conditions that you have to offer. On your travels (or in a picture in a book) you might have seen a magnolia, a particular rose or a green and white variegated bush of scented orange blossom (philadelphus) that caught your fancy. Research this key plant thoroughly. How long does it flower? Are its leaves boring for the rest of the year? Is it only out on your annual summer holiday? Does it need a bog or a frost-free winter to survive? Will it get too big? Does it need sun? That sort of thing. The homework is important, because whatever you choose is going to be the linchpin of the planting scheme. How to plan the smaller plants in a border comes later.

PRACTICALITIES

There are practical considerations too. If you dislike getting your feet wet every time you put the dustbin out, then a path is vital. If there is room for a compost heap, use it for weeds and some grass cuttings in alternate layers. This saves on buying the bulky organic composts and fertilizers that will keep plants healthy and cut down on work. If a pond or swimming pool was all you ever wanted, remember the risks with small children. If you love cooking choose a style of garden where herbs will not look out of place.

You could try drawing all this to see what you have forgotten and how it fits on to the site, but in order to draw an accurate plan you would need a survey. This costs money, but if it can be afforded and if seeing the garden set out on paper helps to focus the mind, it may be worth getting it done. Or you can do it yourself, which will take time, though the principles of surveying are not difficult to grasp. All surveys are based on a series of triangles measured between fixed points in the garden (like the corners of buildings or trees) to wherever you plan a feature. All these lines are recorded and then plotted on graph paper until you have built up a picture of the relationship of everything that exists on the ground, with a record of its measured distance from other existing objects, as well as from the positions of new planned features. A proper survey will mark changes in level as well as the position of major trees and built features. Infinitely cheaper and perfectly acceptable for most people is an enlarged version of the Ordnance Survey map, which shows your house and the shape of its garden. This will be fractionally inaccurate when enlarged because copying machines stretch the proportions of plans or drawings, so it could not be used as part of a proper specification for contractors without checking the measurements. But it

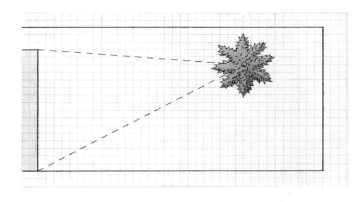

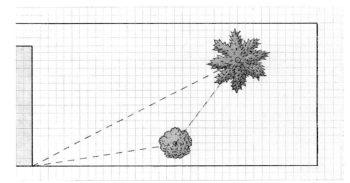

provides an opportunity to think about the shape of the place and the relationships of the spaces and also offers a layout where measurements can be recorded.

For the garden described in the early chapters of this book, we had no proper survey, but only a blown-up map. I have always found this basic information quite enough as a starting point for thinking about the whole concept of any garden. Combined with relentless pacing about out of doors, it will provide plenty of information for a rough plan. To measure with a tape two people are needed, but walking in huge strides, the distance can be counted in paces as you walk. This is useful when you want to draw a flower bed fairly accurately, so as to make a planting plan. It is also important because every time you cover the ground you get nearer to understanding the place and can begin to experiment with setting out the different areas or features in the garden. After the pacing stage you can begin to be more accurate. For those who want a formal garden, a ball of coloured or white string, plenty of canes and three pieces of wood nailed together to form a right-angled triangle will be useful, but for those who favour informality a stout rope or

OPPOSITE: *In Beth Chatto's garden, self-seeded annual honesty looks uncontrived under blossoming apple.*

ABOVE: *Triangulation – using the measurements from two fixed points to find the position of a third – enables you accurately to plot the existing features in your garden on graph paper, and to mark any new features.*

RIGHT: *Formal layouts must be positioned with other structures in mind, and the central point fixed first. The beds can then be measured through the centre in both diagonal and horizontal lines.*

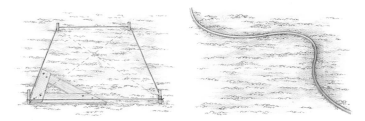

length of hosepipe is easier to manage on the curve. Forget a formal pattern of beds if the ground slopes, unless you can afford to have it terraced; for the final setting out of a formal layout, a tape measure and the perfect triangle are musts. I find it helps to leave the string or the hose arrangement on the ground, so that there is a chance to look at it over several days.

The challenge of making a garden is to create something beautiful in spite of an impossible number of limitations, but the only way to get what you want and will ultimately enjoy is to keep reminding yourself of all the factors which govern your choice and to look at it over and over again until you are happy with the layout. Your eyes and your feet are the best tools at this early stage.

SPACE AND SCALE

A pace is a good human scale measurement for paths. One pace wide (around 90 centimetres) will give you a solo path, too narrow to walk with anyone else, but if you like the

feeling of being crowded and jostled by plants, as I do, you will not mind. Two paces is a more companionable width, but for comfort, an extra 30 centimetres makes all the difference. Paths that are 2 metres wide are perfect for strolling side by side, but not necessarily arm in arm. This was Gertrude Jekyll's preferred dimension; she never liked to walk in front of people in the garden for fear they should be struck by the width of her person. A path three paces wide is spacious but unless you can provide scale vertically, the beds need to be similarly generous. A 3-metre walk between an avenue of trees, or borders that are high, wide and plentiful, will probably work better than the same width of path bordered by ribbon borders of rock plants. In the part of our kitchen garden where the simple flowers grow, I made a wide grass path with a bed and box hedge of a similar size on one side, but did not want to end up with grand double borders under the eye of the church. A narrow bed under the wall has an old damson tree at its centre and pyramid plums, loganberries and blackberries on the wall, with a few flowers under them. The inconsequential treatment was deliberate because I wanted the width of the path to be peaceful and uncrowded by the sweet Williams and old-fashioned flowers that grow next to it. Two borders of equal width would have put more focus on the plants than on the space and quiet which I like here.

How you manipulate space is just as important as how you arrange the plants. Keep asking yourself whether there is enough of it to balance the busy concentrated effects of the flowers. The contrast between light and shade, space and clutter, gives a garden pace and mood. In the end, what satisfies you is what will work best. Two visitors to the garden here in its third summer were critical of the outsize plants in the summer garden. The silver thistles, crambe and angelica seemed to them too large for the beds and the width of the paths, but I love this crowded feeling of being

ABOVE: *An improvised set-square can be used to mark the right-angled corners that are so important for formal beds. A hose or rope is useful for marking informal curves.*

LEFT: *Unless you prefer to walk alone or in single file, a path must be wide enough for two to walk along, even when plants have blurred the edges of the beds.*

LEFT: *This late-summer crowd of flowers is dominated by the long-flowering* Salvia sclarea *var.* turkestanica.

BELOW: *These 'before and after' illustrations show how much difference verticals, in the form of trees, can make to a garden.*

surrounded by plants. I always think children have the best view of a garden, and the verticals – the foxgloves, mulleins, verbenas and hollyhocks – give grown-ups the chance to become children again.

CONTRASTS

Not everyone will share this Alice in Wonderland approach to planting. Those who prefer to look down on groups of flowers at ankle level would feel uneasy amongst the Titans crashing and colliding in the summer beds here. All that matters is that you analyse your aim and that you provide for some contrast to the planted parts of the garden. If jam-tart beds filled with jewel-bright plants in the sun are what you like, plan a tree with nothing under it but green shade to give you a rest and provide the relief that will make the flower beds seem all the brighter by comparison.

When you have finally settled the flat plan of the garden, you will need to add some height. Co-opting people as walking hedges or trees will help with this. Make the hedges walk across your line of vision, holding a cane at the ultimate height of the hedge. Make them move around as trees, waving a long bamboo to show a spread of branches. Remember that one small tree is probably all that most gardens will take, and mark the place where it will not cast shade (unless that is what you want). If you plan a hedge, stake it out with string to represent its top. These verticals will change the space around you and make it feel quite different. At this stage you may despair, but keep going and, if you are uncertain, leave the layout for a few more days before looking at it again. The early stages of making a garden are a bit like choosing the menu for a meal: once you have assembled the ingredients the work is almost done.

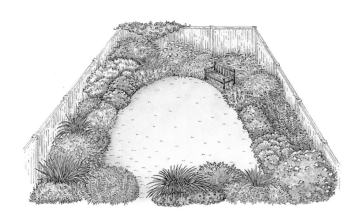

HEAVY AND HARD WORK

The labour of making a garden is heavy and hard and there are times when all of us feel that the effort is too demanding to manage alone. It is sensible to have a plan of campaign before you get to the last limits of exhaustion, otherwise you will end up with the first person that you can grab to finish the job, who may not always be the best. For gardens of the size of our own and smaller I would always prefer to use a contractor who is local to the district and who has worked for years with the soil and materials in the area. There is no advantage in using a large firm; you will only be paying for offices and managers and, in the end, the work will only be as good as the person who actually does it. Try to see something that your contractor has built or laid out recently. If the paving stones look wobbly, the pointing on walls is crude and the turf looks uneven or poor, another search must be made. The good local contractors will tend to be very busy – a three-month wait would not be surprising. Those who can come at the first telephone call are probably not worth having.

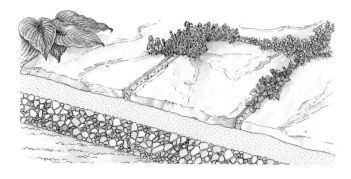

GETTING HELP

The sort of work that you might identify for a contractor to do is laying paving stones and paths, building walls and steps, earth-moving with machinery, tree surgery, drainage and turfing. It is sensible to get two prices for the job, even if you have already decided that the contractor you want to employ is the best on offer. Asking someone else to do the work should not mean the abdication of your interest in the project: it is very important that you have a clear idea of what you want to see, before it is built. Resist all offers of the 'leave it to me, I know exactly what you want' variety until you are certain that the end product will be to your satisfaction. This means asking to see samples of materials before they are bought (or buying them yourself), as well as having some idea of the problems that may arise during each operation.

LAYING PAVING STONES AND PATHS

The hard surfaces in a garden – the paths and sitting places – can prove expensive to install, especially for those who prefer natural to man-made materials. Real stone cut into rectangles of varying sizes for paved areas can be more expensive than the best fitted indoor carpet.

Modern machine-made versions vary in quality, but they do weather in the end. If they are well laid and can be put down in varying sizes, arranged around a keystone, they will look almost real in time. (Ask for 'random' paving.) If the sizes of the stones you choose have to be similar, make sure they are put down with the joints staggered, like brickwork, and not in a continuous line. A mixture of new paving stones with inserted patches of brick can also be an effective way of breaking up bland concrete slabs. Crazy paving leaves the edges of the stone uneven, like pieces of

OPPOSITE AND BELOW: *Brick and tile paths provide attractive, practical surfaces, and make any planting look finished. But hard paths do need to be laid properly.*

ABOVE: *The illustration on the left shows stone slabs that have been left unpointed and laid on a bed of 15-centimetre scalpings (or fine rubble) topped with approximately half that height in sand. To the right of this a gravel path is shown: the base can be a little less deep than for a slab path because it will be topped by a layer of hoggin. This is a mixture of clay and stones with a top-dressing of smaller loose stones rolled into it.*

pleasing. Colours vary from buff through cream to white, and in areas where flint is local there will be some black stones among the rest. It is always cheaper to use local sources, because the cost of transport contributes hugely to the price of gravel, but before placing an order try a handful of the stuff on the path to make sure it will look right in its new surroundings. Look at the stone or brick walls, wooden fencing or colour-washed house to judge whether the gravel chosen is of the same colour tone. If it is not, search for another source until it looks right.

Pea-shingle can be a nuisance on shoes or boots with ridged soles as it can be carried on to flower beds or lawns. But because of the small size of the stones this will do no harm and will probably help with drainage. Indoors, the stones are more irritating, especially if some members of the household dislike changing their shoes. But for beauty, pea-shingle has it every time.

All gravel needs to be laid on good foundations. A 10-centimetre base of rubble or large stones, topped with a 7-centimetre layer of gravel and clay hoggin, will last for years. For a perfect finish and weed-free paths, it also helps to put down an impermeable layer of plastic. This can be an expensively bought proprietary material like Terram or ordinary heavy-duty plastic. Put it between two layers of sand and use fewer of the rubble base stones. The topping of gravel is then rolled into the sticky hoggin surface. Paths made like this can be edged with wooden shuttering to keep the gravel away from flower beds, but I prefer a line of large stones, like flints, as this always looks better and will outlast wood by years. If you do choose shuttering, ask for 10 centimetres by 2.5 centimetres treated softwood timber, with 4-centimetre square pegs. The wood is fixed to the pegs every 1.5 metres and the top edge should be completely level all the way down the side of the path.

broken china. It is often despised but if the pieces of stone are real and large enough, crazy paving can be a very good traditional way of covering areas of ground in the country. Ribbons of cement around it are what make it look unappealing, and it is better for paths or places around doors than for sitting areas, because the stones tend to be too uneven for chairs and tables.

All paving should be laid on at least 15 centimetres of scalpings, or fine rubble topped with 7 centimetres of sand. Some people like to put a dab of cement under each stone to fix it, but if the ground has been well prepared and levelled this is not essential. I prefer the joints left unpointed: if the cracks between the stones are cement-free it looks much friendlier. The joints, which can be as much as about 2 centimetres wide, can be filled with a mixture of grit and sand for carpeting plants, like thyme, to grow. If weeding the paving stones is too much of a chore, the joints can be set closer together.

Where keeping costs down is a priority, gravel may be a better choice than slabs of stone. The smallest washed pea-shingle, which is stones with rounded edges dug from a freshwater pit (rather than chippings from a dry quarry), always looks fresh and tidy. Because these stones are so small, they tend to look more like a single surface than a number of stones. Lightly raked over (in large French gardens this is done every day), nothing looks more

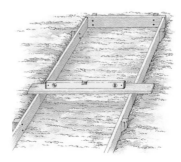

LEFT: *For gravel paths, shuttering made of wooden boards, 10 × 2.5 centimetres, is nailed to 4-centimetre square pegs at 1.5 metre intervals, and checked with a spirit level.*

WALLS AND STEPS

The choice of material for building these should be governed by the materials for the house. Find something that goes happily with what is already on site and you are half-way to success. Walls will need some kind of topping. This might be bricks laid on edge, soldier-fashion, or, on stone walls, a line of upright stones. Coping stones, often in a different material from the wall itself, need to be set at a slope so that water drains away.

Retaining walls (with soil behind them) must always incorporate 'weep-holes' so that the water does not build up at the back and ultimately destroy the wall. Good pointing, which is the mortar joints between the bricks or stones, can make all the difference to the finish, but modern building techniques, with crisp, smooth joints, may not look right in old settings. If you can persuade a contractor to use a grittier lime mortar, rather than a cement mix, and to brush out the joints, instead of finishing them in the approved bucket-handle fashion, they will always look more sympathetic. Advice on using lime mortars is easy to find from conservation organizations, but an all-purpose mixture that I have found useful for contractors who are cement-trained is: 2 parts sharp sand, 2 parts pit or building sand (colours vary; check sands and add stone or brick dust if needed), 1 part lime putty, 1 part HTI or half part snowcrete (hardening agents) – some people substitute 1 part cement for either of these.

OPPOSITE ABOVE: *Even if the effect seems casual, as in this mixture of paving materials, the path must be level.*

ABOVE LEFT: *Walls, paths and other structural features are better built in materials which suit the local area, like this dry stone wall with traditional toppers.*

ABOVE RIGHT: *These chunky stone steps appear less monumental than they might because of the variation in their width and direction.*

BELOW: *Steps made of wooden railway sleepers lead up to a stone wall. In a formal scheme this mix of styles might work less well.*

When it comes to making steps, the wider and shallower they are, the more comfortable they will be. A minimum for the tread is 33 centimetres, which is the largest foot size, and the risers can be anything from 7.5 to 20 centimetres; the stairs inside a house are usually about 15 centimetres high. Although 20 centimetres is steep, sometimes a narrow, steep flight of steps can add drama to a garden. Unless you are trying for a grand Italian layout, avoid straight runs of large numbers of steps, as they can look daunting. A traditional technique used on farm buildings and cottages where space is limited is to set the flight of stairs parallel to the wall that they are climbing; this can be a clever solution in a steep garden. If you cannot visualize what you are about to order, make a mock-up of a couple of steps in brick or stone, so that you can try the proportions out for size. Then stand back and try to imagine what they will look like in their intended position and make sure that they are in scale with their surroundings.

EARTH MOVING

The thought of levels throws amateur garden designers into a panic. If you have had a proper survey made of the garden you will be able to see from this plan how much the levels vary. If no measurement exceeds any other by more than 76 centimetres and, provided there is room, you can probably

ABOVE: *The proportions of steps can be varied, as shown in these illustrations. The wide shallow ones below make for slow walking. Above these a flight with a tread only a little larger than a man's foot and a comfortable rise makes a practical change of level. Steep and narrow steps (top) make a garden seem more of an adventure.*

RIGHT: *This retaining wall blends with the stone of the path and is softened by clumps of rockery plants.*

OPPOSITE ABOVE: *Banks that are retained by a wall will take up less space.*

OPPOSITE BELOW: *Retaining walls can go up in stages as the ferny tier opposite demonstrates.*

get away with a bank, which might be hidden by a wedge of hedge planted at the bottom and top and cut flat on top. Alternatively, you could leave it as a grass bank, or choose to plant it less formally, with a hedge of spreading shrubs. Above this height, a retaining wall will probably be needed, unless there is space for a large bank. At much greater variations in levels, a second terrace or a combination of wall topped by bank are possible solutions. Without a level survey, you can get a rough idea of the changes in height by finding the highest point in the ground. Plant a bamboo cane there and at ground level attach a long piece of string to it. Two people are needed for this job: one to make sure the string is level (with a spirit level) and the other to tie the extended string to the bamboos stuck in to the lower areas. Then measure the distance from this point to the base of the cane. This will give you enough information about the site to discuss the area with the contractor.

Bulldozers or small diggers can shift enormous amounts of soil. Expect to pay around four times the current agricultural wage for the hire of a machine and driver for one day and do not grudge a penny of it, because what it can do will be more than ten men could manage in a week. If you want to end up with a completely level surface, make sure the contractor uses stakes hammered into the ground, with the finished level measured off on to a bar nailed across the stake. Small diggers and dumpers can also be used for ripping out path trenches, old hedges or tree stumps, for carting manure near areas where beds are to be made or for moving piles of stones. It is critical to wait for the ground to be dry before inviting machinery into the garden, or you will end up with compacted soil which will be unworkable. Tracked vehicles do less damage than wheeled ones, but do not be bullied into allowing someone who wants to get on with the job to work on wet ground.

TREE SURGERY

This is best left to the professionals. In conservation areas permission will be needed before any mature tree is felled and the tree surgeon can arrange this. The chosen operator should have some form of approval from a recognized arboricultural association: it is not a job for a cowboy. Once trees have been felled they will need to have the stumps removed because leaving old stumps in the ground is an invitation to honey fungus. This is not a disease to court, as it will attack weak or susceptible plants for years to come and there is as yet no cure for it.

Very large trees will leave a crater behind if their stumps are burnt or carted away, whereas modern stump grinders make an efficient job of chewing up the remains on the spot, leaving a pile of bark chippings for spreading around newly planted shrubs and trees. Access for the stump grinder is an important consideration. The machine is heavy and will damage wet ground, so this is something that needs to be discussed with the tree surgeon before the operation starts to present more problems that it solves. Crown thinning of very large shady trees is worth considering if your garden is dark all day. Even sycamores treated this way can become objects of beauty, and under the thinned canopy it should then be possible to grow a few shade-loving plants.

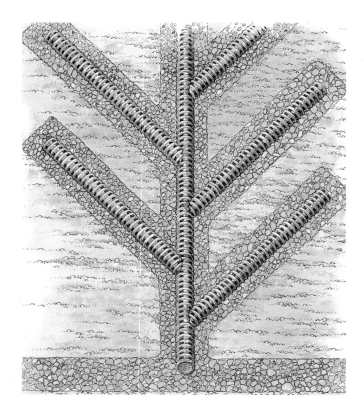

DRAINAGE

If the soil has become compacted, which often happens around new buildings, drainage may be needed. On clay soils, standing water may make it impossible to grow anything. The Ministry of Agriculture (ADAS) operates a consultancy service that gives good impartial advice on this sort of problem. If the water consistently lies in one place, a perforated flexible drainage pipe running underground to the nearest storm-water outlet (not the home waste outlet) is a simple option. The contractor should dig a trench lined with stones and lay the pipe on top of this, cover it with another layer and then bury the whole thing under earth or path. In flower beds, never work wet compacted soil, but as the surface dries, dig in grit and compost to lighten it. Repeated applications of mulch in the form of manure, leaf mould or home-made compost will attract worms to aerate the soil so that it becomes perfectly friable. This process takes about three years and tender plants will be lost in the winter while water-logging is a problem. For those in a hurry, a pattern of drains laid in herringbone fashion under the bed will be quicker, but phenomenally expensive.

TURFING

This is a poor substitute for seeding, as you never quite know what sort of grass you will get. For the best lawns, a mixture without rye grass is essential and this is rarely on offer as turf supplied by small contractors. Sown at the right time, in late spring, and watered assiduously, grass seed can be up and green within a matter of weeks, but if you have to walk on it instantly, turf may be the only option. This will always be more expensive. All lawns need to be perfectly level and firm before sowing or turfing, and this is an operation which needs practice to get it right. If you are the kind of person who could tackle laying a carpet or tiles indoors and end up with a good finish you could probably create a lawn. But it is a job that most people would prefer to give to a professional. After turf has been laid, it should be rolled, and if no rain falls it will need watering. If the gaps between the turfs begin to open, that is a sign that more watering and rolling is needed. Without a roller, careful treading to spread the joints can be tried, but there is a danger that bumps and hollows will be created if the ground is too wet or the tread uneven, so rolling is better.

OPPOSITE: *Drainage can be provided by laying a perforated pipe on a bed of gravel, herringbone fashion. The excess water is carried to a soakaway trench, which is also filled with gravel.*

THIS PAGE: *The fine lawn above needs better quality turf than the meadow grass shown below, where the grass is cut at different lengths to allow bulbs and wildflowers to grow.*

GROUND
WORKS

It is a waste of time and money to put plants into unprepared ground. If you cannot get a large fork into the earth or turn the soil over without swearing, wrecking your back or breaking the fork, then conditions are not ideal. If a mat of weeds covers the ground these must be eradicated. The best and traditional time to do this is all through the winter, when the ground should be dug over roughly and left exposed to the elements. Any visible white roots must be picked out again and again. Couch grass, which has fine thread roots, ground elder with white knobbly roots and bindweed, which looks like spaghetti, will keep recurring if you do not get them out before you plant, and in the end they will choke off the expensive newcomers. This is a counsel of perfection. Even the best dug plots may still have weeds after a winter of work on land in poor condition. But followed up with weedkiller, as they start to grow in spring and before planting, they will disappear. Rotovating is not a good idea as it chops perennial weeds into small pieces and leaves their roots in the ground.

Those who cannot bear the thought of poisoning can adopt various green measures to clean a plot after winter digging. Before weedkillers became available, gardeners always gave the ground a summer planting of an annual crop to be certain of a weed-free site. Potatoes are often used to clear ground that has been uncultivated for years, but any annual, whether vegetable or flower, will give you the chance to see what emerges in the first season, before a second thorough dig in the winter months. When permanent plants like shrubs or perennials are planted in places where tiny fragments of ground elder or bindweed remain, their roots are likely to become infested, so that the problem spreads out under safe cover of the new plants and rapidly becomes impossible to eradicate.

Another green option after winter digging is to leave the area fallow for a summer, so that weeds can be dug out and hoed off as they appear, but this is hard and dull work. A heavy mulch which blankets the ground is just as effective and much less exhausting. This can be anything that shuts out light – newspapers, plastic or old carpets will do the job – but I prefer to spread a thick 10-centimetre layer of sterilized compost or bark over the whole area. Then if any weeds do emerge they are easy to pull out.

If you cannot wait until winter and want to start to make a garden in the spring or summer months there are ways to do this too. Weedkiller applied in the growing season is the fastest route to clearing a bed of persistent perennials like ground elder or bindweed. Use Roundup or Tumbleweed, which only kills growing plants and does not last in the soil. This takes about three weeks to work. For tough numbers like docks, you may have to repeat the operation, but weedkiller will never turn a flower bed into loose crumbly soil that can be planted without delay, and as digging some soils in summer, when they are baked clay, is a physical impossibility, you will have to cheat if you want immediate results. Luckily, plants from the garden centre arrive in their own living quarters, which will last them for a month or two. By the time they begin to reach beyond their container environment you should have conditioned the soil into a more suitable state to receive their roots. This can be done by spreading a thick layer of whatever you can afford over the ground and between the new plants. Using grass cuttings (from a neighbour, if you do not have a lawn) is one possibility. Chopped bark from the garden centre is a more expensive one, but it lasts longer than other materials. Peat, if you can stand the ecological irresponsibility, is another. An 8-centimetre layer of any of these will soon improve the consistency of the soil and repel weeds but will not enrich it. As the mulching materials decompose, they deprive the earth of nitrogen, so if the new plants are not to starve they will need feeding with a balanced fertilizer. Well-rotted manure, which can be bought in bags but is cheaper from a local farmer by the load, is useful stuff for spreading on new beds, because it feeds as well as conditions the soil. Mushroom compost, lighter and cleaner to handle than manure, will also enrich the ground, but its lime content tends to be high, so on limy soils, years of use can lead to problems. I find it invaluable, but try to use chopped bark, instead of mushroom compost, one season in three to correct the acid balance. Bark from pines is particularly good for this. Home-made compost or leaf mould are the best and cheapest of all soil-conditioning mixtures.

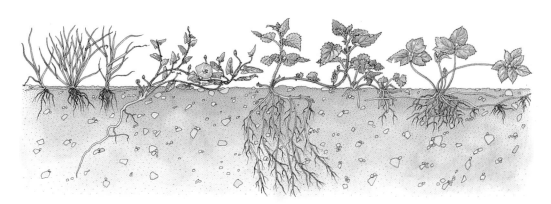

OPPOSITE: *Borders like these can be achieved only by preparing the ground well before planting, which means eradicating all perennial weeds.*

LEFT: *The worst perennial weeds are (from left to right): couch grass, bindweed, nettle, creeping buttercup and ground elder.*

TOP-DRESSING AND COMPOSTS

It is impossible to overstress the importance of clean, well-nourished ground to give plants a good start in life. The final aim is weed-free crumbly soil which looks dark and rich and is a pleasure to dig. The route to this is via your chosen organic material, which you keep piling on to the plot or bed every year. Even clay soils, which are back-breakers and fork-wreckers, can be improved by barrow loads of manure or compost. Light sandy soils that drain quickly will also benefit from years of top dressing because they will hold water better if you can build up their texture

with leaf mould, manure or compost after the initial process of removing deep perennial weeds. Very little digging needs doing in beds with permanent plants. The worms will do it all for you if you give them plenty of organic matter to pull down into the soil. All soils, even the worst clay or the thinnest and stoniest, can be improved in a couple of years by barrow loads of organic mulch.

It makes sense to make your own soil conditioner in a compost heap. Make a pile of vegetable waste in a corner of the garden, where it will rot down to something that looks like the blackest of fruit cakes. This can include annual weeds, lawn mowings, leaves, straw, wood ash and plants that get cut down after a summer, as well as kitchen waste. Whole books have been written about the making of compost, but you can achieve what you want with minimum fuss in a proprietary bin. Where there is space you can do as we did and have them custom built. Three heaps is the ideal number, but we have two side by side, retained with wooden rails, because we have so much recyclable rubbish. They are not turned, but when one is full, it is covered and occasionally watered until the heap looks ready to use after the worms have got to work. This takes about nine months to a year. The process can be faster if heaps are turned and built up in scientific layers, but our system works well enough for our purposes.

ABOVE: *This compost heap is divided in two. The side with straw will take a while to rot but the other heap is perfect to crop courgettes and can be barrowed around the roots of ornamentals, once the marrows have finished.*

LEFT: *Hedges are the backbone of a garden. Here they furnish a space without any flowers.*

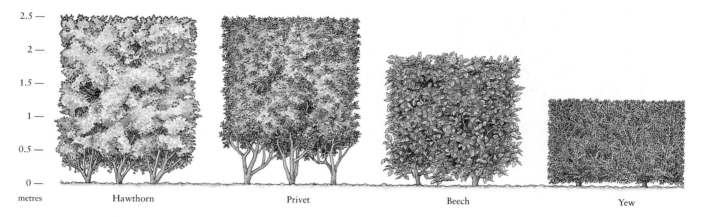

2.5 —
2 —
1.5 —
1 —
0.5 —
0 —
metres   Hawthorn   Privet   Beech   Yew

PLANTING THE FRAMEWORK

Once the ground is in a fit state to receive plants you can begin to put them in. For shrubs and trees, it is worth taking the extra trouble to dig out a planting pit (or for hedges a trench) at least 90 centimetres wide and as deep as you can manage: about 30 centimetres below the root ball of whatever it is you plan to plant is ideal. Add manure or compost and if you cannot find these, buy soil conditioner and add some extra fertilizer (this might be peat or cocoa fibre, boosted by blood, fish and bone). Mix any of these into the earth at the bottom of the pit and add a handful of bonemeal. Even when the new large permanent plants are in, there can be no let-up in the clean-well-nourished-ground rule. In the first years of their life, the more weeding, watering and feeding new hedges, trees and shrubs receive, the better they will prosper. Evergreen hedges of the most expensive sort are always thought to be slow to mature, but yew and box will grow from 20 to 30 centimetres a year with proper treatment. Planted in a well-prepared trench, watered in dry periods and fed with a balanced fertilizer like Vitax Q4 in spring and again at midsummer, they should do well. If they are also given booster doses of high nitrogen in the form of dried blood at three-week intervals they will put on phenomenal growth. Spare the time to do this for three seasons, and it will give the hedges, which will be the backbone of your planting, a proper start in life and make you the envy of neighbours who have planted quick-growing x *Cupressocyparis* or lonicera for their evergreen walls. After five years the 'get-hedged-quick' brigade will have to cut their *leylandiis* three or four times a season, but as box and yew need only an annual trim, you will

BELOW: *Hedges, like trees, rearrange the volume of space. With plenty of feeding and weeding, this beech arch might be achieved in about seven years.*

ABOVE: *This illustration compares the different rates of growth of various hedging plants put in at about 30 centimetres high, after about four years.*

save many more hours in a summer than were spent in the early years on nursing them through their infancy.

Most deciduous hedges do get away more quickly than the noble evergreens, but they too will respond to loving care by growing thick and fast. As a general rule, the faster a hedge naturally grows, the more it will have to be cut. Beech is slower than privet or thorn, but will grow to the

garden, which is classified as part of the fixtures and fittings attached to the house that you leave behind. Like the mulberry that we brought with us to the gooseberry garden, any plant can be excluded from this list, provided the buyer has notice of your intentions. Large trees like ours need preparing a year ahead of the move, by digging a trench under the outermost branches all round the tree. This is then filled with compost or manure to encourage the feeding roots that will be needed to help the plant survive being uprooted. A tree of between 3 and 4 metres high is probably about as large as can be manhandled out of its hole on to sacking or plastic sheeting and into a barrow or truck. Anything larger would be better tackled by a tree spade, but in small gardens access for large tree-lifting machines is usually non-existent, so unless you have room for heavy machinery to manoeuvre, forget moving anything much larger than our mulberry.

Some plants are notoriously bad movers. All the quick-growing shrubs like buddleja, ceanothus, cytisus, cistus, lavenders, rosemaries and salvias (and this is not an exhaustive list) hate being transplanted. Nor do roses enjoy it much, but as all these things grow fast I would rarely think it worth the trouble of trying to persuade them to put down roots a second time. In any new garden rearranging what seemed like a good idea at the time, to a place that you now believe to be perfect, is a constant process. If you do want to move shrubs or trees, the dormant season is the only possible time. Just as you would do when planting new acquisitions, prepare a pit for the transplants with plenty of friable compost or manure (which should never be fresh), water and feed them regularly in their first season after moving and, if they seem reluctant to come into leaf, spray their leaves with water three times daily, as we did with the mulberry tree, and they should survive.

Smaller shrubs and herbaceous plants are also better moved in the months when they have ceased to grow, but some perennials are fussy about moving in spring and some do not like being lifted in autumn. Peonies rarely settle after a spring upheaval, but the daisy tribe prefer to wait until spring to make new roots. If in doubt, reference books provide invaluable guidance. Looking things up is not an admission of defeat; there are very few people who can remember how to please all the plants in cultivation.

height of a man in about four to five years if carefully tended and will need cutting only twice a year, rather than the three or four sessions needed to keep privet looking trim. The size of plants when you buy them is also an important factor. Choose bushy plants in preference to taller ones and do not be depressed if your purse will not stretch to large specimens. The smaller the plant, the faster it grows, and the easier it is to look after. Yew planted at around 30 to 46 centimetres will often catch up plants put in at 90 to 120 centimetres. Large plants of evergreens are expensive to buy and often stand still in the first year of planting, whereas smaller versions will be less traumatized by their move and will settle to growing straight away.

MOVING PLANTS

Some plants move better than others. Sometimes, as we did, new gardeners want to take plants with them when they go. Under English law you are not allowed to remove the

Many plants do not mind being moved, as long as the timing is right. Roses (opposite) *will support a change in winter, when they are dormant. Peonies* (right) *prefer an autumn shift but asters insist on spring. Most herbs, like purple sage* (below), *will not enjoy any change of position.*

ACQUISITIONS

New plants also need careful treatment during the transition from nursery or garden centre to their ultimate resting place. In summer, pot-grown plants are easier to establish than bare-rooted ones, which are available only in the dormant season and are much cheaper to buy. For this reason I prefer to plant trees and hedges as bare-root stock bought direct from the nursery that grows them, rather than from a garden centre. Although pot-grown specimens can be planted at any time of the year, they will rarely out-perform plants which have had the chance to settle into their new positions in autumn. In winter their roots should never be exposed to frost, so whether bare-rooted or in pots, stand them in a shed, or wrap them well in newspaper and fleece, if you cannot plant them straight away. When the ground is frozen hard, you may have to keep them waiting, but they will come to no harm if they are protected for a few weeks. If you have no time to plant properly in the winter months and the ground is workable, the best place to store new arrivals is in a shallow trench, where you lay the plants sideways and cover their roots with a good layer of earth. In summer, shade is vital for new plants in pots and they will need to be watered. One of the saddest sights for a committed gardener is to find a row of unhappy acquisitions wilting in the sun as they wait to be planted.

BORDERS

The best place for a border to grow flowers is obviously the sunniest and most sheltered that can be spared, and the backing of a wall, fence or hedge is ideal. Gardeners who are bent on curves may like the idea of island beds that float in a sea of lawn. They are, however, much harder to arrange than those which are viewed only from the front and the side. A decent depth for a flower bed is 1.5 metres out from a wall, but the wider the border, the easier it will be to create a long-lasting display from different sorts of plants.

Narrow beds – 1 metre and under – are less good for a mixture of flowers, but are brilliant places for planting one-at-a-time features. For example, if you wanted a permanently planted sunny narrow bed you might put in clumps of pinks, which have silver leaves all winter, and small flowers like carnations that are very scented in June and July. As well as these, you could grow tulips. These would flower in the spring to be followed by patches of a sparse-growing bright blue flax (*Linum perenne*), which carries on for most of the summer. If there was a wall or a fence at the back, that could provide support for a rose and perhaps a clematis as well. There would never be a great blast of colour, but a succession of well-chosen flowers can be just as rewarding as a box of bedding plants and in the long run cheaper and less work.

PLANTING STYLES

When it comes to planning a wider flower bed, there are several ways of organizing it. The first task is to narrow down the choice of plants by deciding what kind of effect you are trying to create. It may be that, after visiting other gardens or consulting gardening books, you have formed an idea of what you would like to see dominating the flower bed. Or you might want to devote an area to one season of the year, to a colour theme, or to a collection of plants that complement one another. At an early stage, it is also important to decide on the style of planting. Formal beds can be contained with a unifying edge of the same plant. Repeated clumps are another way of achieving formality and are good if you want to reinforce a colour theme. A romantic muddle of flowers tumbling into one another is right for cottage schemes. How much work you can manage will also influence the arrangement. Traditional perennials

OPPOSITE: *Bulbs provide bold blocks of colour in these formal beds.*

ABOVE: *In this border, which is devoted to herbs, the repeated towers of hops create a formal structure above low informal plants, and give the bed the feeling of an avenue.*

RIGHT: *Borders come in many styles and places. These traditional roses and summer flowers are planted on an almost vertical slope.*

LEFT: *This border relies on the repetition of clumps of plants such as dahlias to give it unity.*

BELOW AND OPPOSITE: *In narrow flower beds, unity becomes even more important. This scheme shows a rose planted against the wall with a solanum growing through it. In spring the bed has tulips behind clumps of pinks. There are two waves of tulips, with the early crimson form 'Couleur Cardinal' followed by the later green and white 'Spring Green', which appears as the dianthus and the solanum begin to flower. Later, a cloud of the blue flax,* Linum narbonense, *takes over with the rose 'New Dawn'. The season finishes with the crimson clematis 'Gravetye Beauty'. All year, the silver-grey leaves of the dianthus, which need constant renewal, furnish the bed.*

have to be lifted and divided if they are to flower well, and some of them may need staking to stop them falling over. If you cannot give them the attention they need it is not worth the attempt to grow them. In fact, if you cannot grow a plant well it is better to leave it alone. Gardens where rarities hang on to life by one stem are gloomy places.

PLANTING SCHEMES

Whatever the decision, the process is the same. Begin by choosing the most important plants, the linchpins of the scheme. As an example of how this might work, imagine that the chosen formula for a border is to make it full of flowers all summer and easy to manage. The linchpin might be the pale pink tree mallow *(Lavatera* 'Barnsley') which will grow to about 1.5 metres high and almost as wide. A little research will reveal that it flowers non-stop from July until the frosts, so plants are needed for the early part of the year when the lavatera is not performing. You need, too, to think about what sort of colours will go with the pale pink of the mallow if they are going to be out together. It helps to make a list of likely candidates, with the time that they flower and then to group these under seasons, so that you can see when there will be gaps without flowers. If you always take a holiday at the same time of year you may want to ignore flowers for that month. Putting it down on paper helps with the organization of a spread of interest throughout the summer.

Spring

Early summer

Having planned the sequence, you then turn to plotting the space. Draw a rough plan on squared paper that is in scale with the border, so that you can see how much room each plant will occupy. Block in the squares each one will need when fully grown. You may find you have far too much on the seasonal interest list and will need to reduce it again. The best borders are a mixture of perennials, shrubs, bulbs and a few tender plants or annuals, but because there is so much suitable material, it is easier to make a few rules that restrict your choice. Forget difficult plants at the start, unless either you can offer them what they crave or you have money to burn. Leave others to grow the alpines that demand perfect drainage, or the camellias that hate lime, or the daphnes that are prone to virus diseases. Make sure that under and around the linchpins the colours are working as

Planting a narrow bed

1 *Dianthus* 'Gran's Favourite'
2 *Dianthus* 'Haytor White'
3 *Dianthus* 'Laced Monarch'
4 *Dianthus* 'Becky Robinson'
5 *Linum narbonense*
6 *Clematis* 'Gravetye Beauty'
7 *Rosa* 'New Dawn'
8 *Solanum crispum* 'Glasnevin'

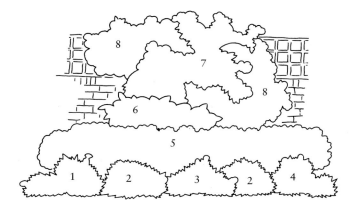

Late summer

you want them to, so that you rule out everything which is not in a colour you have selected. Then fill in between these areas with large clumps of old favourites. There are two good reasons for starting with unambitious plants, rather than rarities. Easy plants are good for morale because they grow fast and they tend to be cheap – and are sometimes free. Established gardens often have a surplus of perennials to give away and it is worth asking neighbours in the autumn or in spring, when plants are being divided, if there are any to spare. Most gardeners are generous with encouragement and hate throwing things away. The chances are that new gardeners will come away with all sorts of bounty, as well as good local advice. Most people can spare plants like hardy geraniums, alchemilla and catmint. These are invaluable at the start of a border because they gallop across the ground and, when the first summer is over, they can be lifted to leave spaces for rarer plants or they can be increased to fill other gaps. Bulbs are rewarding and infallible. Cheer up the first spring with tulips or narcissi and follow them perhaps with irises if the border is sunny. Add the hardy geraniums and catmint, until the roses and perhaps the green-flowered ladies' mantle (*Alchemilla mollis*) take over, and end the year with the 'Barnsley' mallow. As you get more confident you can start introducing other less common plants.

If flowers are not your style, leafscapes, where the shape and texture of the plants are more important than their flowers, are an alternative way of furnishing a border. Choose an evergreen for winter as the linchpin and build a group of plants around it, picking sometimes spiky and sometimes rounded leaves, with others that look as though they are made of fine filigree and yet more that seem to have been precision-carved. The best plantings draw on both these styles, using a mixture of colour and form. Composing pictures from leaves and flowers is difficult, because you are working with different heights and widths, as well as being dependent on time to produce the effect you want. You will find that when you start to plant a permanent scheme the bulbs will be perfect their first year and that some perennials will grow much faster than others. Almost all perennials will double in size before the shrubs get going. Unlike the herbaceous plants, shrubs will be difficult to move if they are too close together when mature.

Early summer:
Ceanothus 'Edinburgh', *Erysimum* 'Bowles' Mauve', tulips 'China Pink' (quite bright with 'Bowles' – would 'Queen of Night' (very dark purple) be better?). Add *Allium* 'Purple Sensation' throughout. Irises?

Midsummer:
Rosa 'Zéphirine Drouhin' (shocking pink – is rose 'Climbing Iceberg' better?), delphiniums, cistus, peony, nepeta, alchemilla.

Late summer:
Lavatera 'Barnsley', anemones (both these are pale), perovskia (blue – good shape), *Clematis* 'Jackmanii', delphinium. These last two are strong purple and blue – should colours be all subdued, or mixed dark and pale? Is shocking pink 'Zéphirine' too strong in late summer? Would more late colour from, say, *Origanum* 'Herrenhausen' be better than iris foliage and early flowers?

Early summer

Midsummer

When you draw the first version of a planting plan, it helps to set it out on graph paper allowing four squares to represent a metre. Unless you have an exceptional visual sense, which can operate both in time and space, you will need to make notes around the plan to remind you of how the flowers will change with the season. In this simple plan for summer colour the notes might read as on the page opposite. These notes help to focus the mind. As the season progresses, more can be added and changes made.

Planting plan

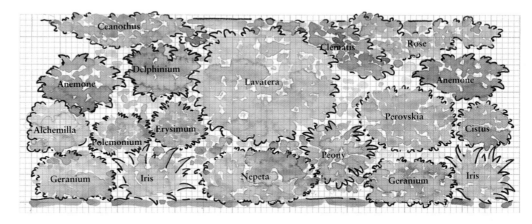

Late summer

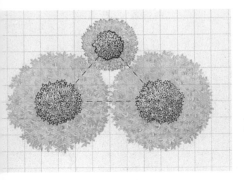

This drawing illustrates how to space plants. Put them as far apart as they will be when mature, which means allowing half the final width of each plant between the centres.

Shrubs and trees need to be put in so that, at their final spacing, they will not crowd each other. As a rough rule, everything should be planted as far from its neighbour as the combined half-widths of each plant. When two of a kind are growing next to one another this formula is easy. Imagine a group of shrubs that will each end up as bushes 1.8 metres wide: they should go in 1.8 metres apart. But if next to this shrub you wanted a plant that would, when mature, occupy only 0.8 metre of lateral space, the distance between the larger and smaller plant would be 1.3 metres.

This leaves you with a problem of what to do in the area between immature shrubs. The cheap and easy standby perennials will certainly cover the ground, but may threaten the growth of the plant that you ultimately want to see. For filling gaps, annuals are sometimes more useful. In the first summer they can provide a tremendous boost for morale. Their root systems are less likely to encroach on the important features in a border, but they will involve more work and expense because they will have to be raised from seed and planted out. Cleverly used, annuals will provide the height and colour that the new linchpins and the standby perennials will take time to achieve. However you furnish the border between the important linchpins, you must remember to leave a breathing space around them, so that they can grow into the strongest features in the scheme.

DIFFICULT AREAS

Problem places need to be tackled with more cunning than well-prepared borders. You can be artistic in shade or in bone-dry places: even heavy clay and chalk have their advantages, but if deep rich loam has not been achieved, your choices will be more restricted. You must respect the prevailing conditions. In thin, sunny, well-drained soils, roses and peonies will struggle, but Mediterranean shrubs and lovely perennials like many of the hardy geraniums, scabious, gaura, eryngiums and iris will thrive. In damp plots, hydrangeas, primulas, aconitums, campanulas and narcissi will grow immeasurably better than anywhere else. The worst place of all to garden is in the dry shade under a tree. You can cheat a little by thinning and raising the canopy of branches; you can even raise the soil level by making a low retained bed around the trunk. Then you might expect a brave show of flowers like cyclamen, snowdrops, aconites and primroses in spring, followed by ferns, foxgloves and more cyclamen for autumn. The challenge of finding plants that will thrive against all odds can be rewarding. Acanthus, *Iris foetidissima* 'Citrina',

LEFT: *Some sites dictate the choice of plants. In damp places plants such as these gunnera and candelabra primulas will thrive.*

OPPOSITE ABOVE: *Exotic tropical plants are seen here in a south coast seaside garden where half-hardy sun lovers thrive.*

Smyrnium perfoliatum, Anemone blanda and *A.nemorosa* are some of the more distinguished plants to try in this most difficult of sites. If one thing does well, encourage it. The sight of a rug of cyclamen in shocking pink under a leafless tree is far more valuable than a scattered covering of odds and ends later in the year.

Too steep to weed and too vertical to retain moisture, banks are another challenge. Something that covers the ground densely and fast is usually the answer. Start the plants small and choose them carefully so that they are bound to succeed. In shade, ivy and periwinkles, especially smaller-leaved sorts, are not to be despised. In sun, the whole range of Mediterranean shrubs will be at your disposal. In all of the problem areas that lie beyond the perfectly prepared 'best places', there may be little that you can do to improve the ground. Trying to grow plants in inhospitable surroundings is a battle that you will never win. Arm yourself with the best book on your conditions, so that you become an expert on chalk, drought, wind or acid bog and plan your campaign accordingly, so that you garden with and not against the terrain.

BELOW: *This illustration shows how the difficult dry area under a tree might be planted with flowers that are woodlanders by choice.*

In winter and spring the ground under a tree can be lovely, especially if early bulbs like snowdrops, aconites and cyclamen are used.

Planting under a tree
1 *Alchemilla mollis*
2 *Digitalis purpurea albiflora*
3 *Mahonia aquifolium*
4 *Polypodium vulgare*
5 *Vinca minor* 'Argenteovariegata'
6 *Daphne laureola*
7 *Polystichum setiferum divisilobum*
8 *Iris foetidissima* 'Citrina'
9 *Daphne pontica*
10 *Asplenium scolopendrium*
11 *Vinca minor* 'La Grave'

A Time-scale for a New Garden

Creating a new garden is a slow haul if you are going to do it yourself. If gardening is to be a pleasure and not a chore you have to be realistic about what you can achieve. This means separating new works from annual management and organizing the former to suit the latter. The winter months are the best time for major alterations and any pruning that has to be done. Reserve the summer for grass cutting, weeding, watering, feeding and judicious pruning or you will end the year exhausted. The building works – the laying of paths and paving, putting up structures to support plants or wiring the walls for climbers, planting hedges, shrubs and trees, the preparing of neglected ground and carting manure – should all be finished by the end of February, or sooner if possible. Many old hedges or shrubs can be renovated by radical pruning in the dormant months (but evergreens are better left until the sap begins to rise). Clearing out hedges and mulching around newly planted trees and shrubs will also give you a good start. What is not finished in the winter must be left until next autumn.

THE BASICS

For those who prefer to phase the work over a few years, the best advice is to start by planting the framework of the garden, and leave the hard landscaping until the second winter. The trees and hedges that will form the background to the flowers you want to grow should be planted as soon as possible. A compost heap is also an early priority because it will save you time on rubbish disposal and money on soil-conditioning mixtures. If you can manage to start work on defeating perennial weeds like ground elder, bindweed, nettles or couch grass, sooner is better than later.

In the first summer, whatever hedges, shrubs and trees you have planted will need constant care. Weed them, feed them, water them and watch them – weekly if you can. Mulching is the shortest cut to no weeding and minimal watering that I know, but it needs to be applied to moist soil just as the ground is warming up in spring. If the new plants are fed with a slow-release fertilizer like Osmocote and then tucked in with a blanket of manure, bark or mushroom compost, they should last for two or three months without much attention. If it is very dry, they will need water, but 7 centimetres of mulch usually keeps things cool in a normal year. Sawdust, spent hops or lawn mowings are all possible materials for mulching. Much more expensive are the manufactured mat mulches that landscapers use; these can be made from paper, wool or man-made fibres. I dislike them because, although they suppress weeds, they do not put anything back into the ground. Permaculturists, who strive to create a mutually sustainable environment in their plots, go for carpets picked off skips, but any carpet that is not an eyesore might be better placed indoors.

PRACTICAL ROUTES

Where funds or labour are in short supply, some of the hard paths can wait for a second winter, until you see where they are most needed. The daily route to the car, the dustbins and the compost heap may be obvious, but the best way to the winter flowers or the shortest cut to a sheltered seat will emerge only in time. Where the grass gets scuffed to death in the cold months you will need to find a long-term solution if you are not to waste valuable time on repairing it each year. (A commitment to grass in heavy-duty areas always involves more maintenance than hard paths.) Places like the gateway to our kitchen garden, where the

OPPOSITE: *It is the structure of the plants that last through winter that takes time to establish. If time is short, give up the flowers in the first season, in favour of weeding, feeding and watering what will be the backbone of the garden. You need the green framework in the cold months much more than summer colour.*

RIGHT: *Any new garden can have annuals, like these poppies, in its first summer.*

The struggle to grow difficult plants in artistic combinations can cause despair. Simple effects like daisies and dandelions in long grass (left), *or plenty of easy to raise alchemilla* (opposite), *lining the path, can often be just as rewarding.*

central path is green, can be perennial problems because bottlenecks like this do not stand up to winter traffic. If you are, as I am, determined to keep the grass, think of the problems it will cause forever. In subsequent winters you may need to use boards in the wettest weather to spread the load. Sometimes it may be enough to stab the ground with a fork in spring to let the air into the compacted soil, but you will always need to find an alternative route while the grass recovers. If the grass fails to grow, returfing would be a possibility, but that would probably cost around the price of four rose bushes for a couple of paces squared and take a morning of valuable labour at a time when there is plenty to do. A technical trick used in large gardens open to the public is to lay turf that has been sown into a textile backing; this seems to last longer than ordinary turf. But for those who want to keep the work down, hard surfaces for the most used areas are vital.

GRASS

While you can defer the hard paths, you will probably want a grassed area for the first summer. Anyone who can afford to have turf laid professionally may also be in a position to get the lawn mown. The rest of the world probably prefers to keep lawn maintenance to a minimum. Rye grass, which is included in lawns recommended for heavy duty (that means football played by ten-year-olds) is beastly to maintain because it makes tough stems that lie parallel to the ground. If there is not too much football in your life,

you should choose a mixture of fine grasses that includes creeping fescues. Never cut it lower than 2 centimetres (but 2.5 centimetres is better), and decide from the start that you like daisies, self-heal, clovers and mosses in the lawn, or you will spend far too much time poisoning and fertilizing. Lawn care is very time-consuming. An emerald sward would be lovely, but never my priority.

Because new gardens are very demanding, tackle only as much as you can manage to encourage and cherish during a year. Bear in mind that lawn grass will probably need to be cut once a week from late March to October, around thirty times a year, and if you want to look in control, tidy edges are essential. Allow ten to fifteen minutes every ten days for each 9 metres of trimming. Because you have to adjust the angle of the shears, uneven edges take longer to manage. Correcting them by an annual slice of the lawn with the half-moon cutter only means that you will end up with less grass and more flower bed than originally planned, so if you can afford to lay wooden boards 7 to 10 centimetres deep along the turf, it will speed up the work with the shears. Bricks or paving, set just under where the grass ends, will also help with keeping things tidy. In theory, the mower runs over the stone, cutting the grass as it does, but in practice this tends to work better with a rotary mower. Even then, the occasional strim may be needed.

Long grass – the place for bulbs in spring – is usually cut with the mower blades set as high as they will go: 7 to 10 centimetres would be about right. This might need half a dozen cuts a year. The first will be the worst, as you have to wait for six weeks after the last bulbs have flowered. Longer grass where wild flowers follow the bulbs, as in our orchard, needs three cuts a year. The first one cannot be made until the meadow flowers have seeded, which can be as late as July, then all the cut grass must be carried away. If you leave it, it will enrich the meadow too much for the wild flowers: they always do better on poor grassland. In order to encourage cowslips and to enjoy the earliest small bulbs, the grass has to be short at the start of winter. The cowslips need winter light to flourish and the crocus and scillas will never be seen if the grass is too long.

FLOWERS

Where resources are stretched, in the first summer of a new garden, you could sow annual flowers combined with vegetables in the flower beds around the one or two linchpin shrubs that you have managed to plant. Try blue cornflowers, parsley, coloured lettuces, ruby chard, borage and mignonette, with the best scented sweet pea, the old-fashioned *Lathyrus odoratus*, for the smell. You could add a few petunias for more rich colour and scent, and even if the bed was not perfectly weed-free you would have an enjoyable summer eating the vegetables and admiring the flowers before tackling the weeds over the second winter. Devising simple schemes with annuals like this one should satisfy the frustrated gardener and encourage the less committed through the hard early stages.

For those who can face the work and like the idea of saving money, the first season is also the time to start raising plants in a nursery bed. Some plants, like campanulas, aquilegias, salvias, hemerocallis and delphiniums, are expensive to buy, but easy to raise from seed. Others, like nepeta, alchemilla, hardy geraniums, achilleas, asters and

ABOVE: *Nursery beds can be used to grow expensive plants from seed or cuttings in great quantities.*

BELOW: *Flower beds can be filled with stop-gap annuals or easy-spreading herbs, like marigolds and marjoram.*

phlox, can be begged or bought and fattened into clumps over a summer, so that they are ready to divide into several plants the following spring. Roses, buddlejas, perennial wallflowers, pinks, lavender, rosemaries and cistus can be grown from cuttings without any special equipment. Line them out in a sandy trench in summer, keep them watered, and by the following spring they should have rooted. These lists are not exhaustive.

CLIMBERS AND SHRUBS

Any existing climbers, as well as those planted in the first year, will need tying and pruning. All climbers are hard work, so if you are daunted by the scope of your project do not plant too many at once, and if ladders are not your idea of fun, avoid large climbers like wisteria and rampant roses. They will need at least a couple of hours' attention from the top rung two or three times a year. Choose instead the self-clingers, like *Hydrangea anomala* subsp. *petiolaris* for shady places, or trachelospermum for a warm wall. Closely clipped bushes of evergreens, like ceanothus or pyracantha, that will support twiners such as clematis or honeysuckle and can be managed from step-ladder height, are another easy option. You can always add climbing roses later, when there is time to spare for managing them. They grow very fast. In the first year, spring-flowering shrubs that have been inherited may also need attention. As a rough rule, anything that flowers before midsummer should have the wood that has flowered cut out as soon as the flowers fade. The new growth will bear next year's blooms. Forsythia, lilac, philadelphus – all the old favourites – will become woodier and less productive with age if they are not regularly pruned. They can be cut back in winter, but you will lose a season's flowers, or the work could be phased so that you tackle half the bush at a time in the dormant season. No harm will come of either of these courses. It is even possible to do nothing for a season or two, until the dead wood becomes too oppressive and all that remains are a few flowers at the top of the bush.

In the first season, after grass care, weeding, watering and feeding of the newly planted areas are the priorities. Allow no weeds to seed, not even groundsel. Around new trees make sure grass keeps its distance, so that each woody plant has 30 to 60 square centimetres of clean ground around it. If it becomes dry under the mulch after ten days without rain, watering will be critical. Feed plants either at the start of the growing season with slow-release Osmocote, which lasts all summer, or with Vitax Q4 every six weeks. The assiduous will add, at fortnightly intervals, a liquid foliar feed in one of the new hose-dilutor bottles. I like to use both a slow-release and a foliar feed to encourage new plants, but only until mid August otherwise growth is too soft to cope with the colder weather ahead. Watering duty can diminish when the dews start. If the work of establishing a new garden appals you, think of using contractors for clearing long grass and cutting established hedges in the first few seasons, because the work for the home team will never be so hard again. With each year the work will diminish. But it is important to consolidate what has already been done before embarking on another phase of work which will attract more maintenance.

LEFT: *Ceanothus is a speedy climber, but needs pruning when the flowers fade to keep growth within bounds. This shrub makes a good host for late-flowering clematis if you can arrange some shade around their roots.*

ABOVE: *Climbing roses are quick and will cover a pergola in a couple of years if they are properly treated. Tall biennials, like foxgloves, make up for a lack of height in a new garden until other plants grow.*

MAINTAINING
THE GARDEN

Maintenance is the key to a lovely garden. The best designer in the world can suggest a layout and a planting plan, but without some commitment to upkeep, there will be nothing to show for it a year later.

As the garden matures, the pleasures should outweigh the chores, but stick to the rule about completing winter work to leave the summer free for the jobs that have to be done to keep the garden looking good. Carry on mulching every year because it will save you hours of weeding and watering. Weeds that do appear are easy to pull out from mulched ground. In the kitchen garden try to hoe before the weeds appear. You should be able to clean 9 square metres in less than an hour every ten days. Between raspberries, beans and peas, a mulch will save you having to hoe.

FEEDING

Most plants will benefit from an annual top dressing of soil improver. Fast-growing Mediterranean shrubs are probably best grown undernourished as it makes them hardier.

Regular feeding will, however, be needed for plants that are known to be greedy. The roses, peonies, dahlias and delphiniums should have whatever formula you have come to trust. Some people swear by seaweed extracts because they repel aphids, others use high nitrogen for bedding plants and many people use tomato fertilizer for everything. My personal proven favourites are dried blood for evergreens, Vitax Q4 and Maxicrop. I often have to resort to rose fertilizers here for the added magnesium which this soil lacks, because rose leaves and box hedges tend to turn yellow when they run short of magnesium. A cheaper solution is Epsom Salts, but granular fertilizers are quicker. Ask good gardeners locally what suits your soil and act on their advice because what works in some places will not suit others so well. If you cannot spare time for feeding individual plants, rely on a spring spread of manure or compost, or a slow-release fertilizer. A more ecological garden than ours, full of native plants that do well locally, or those garden plants which will survive in unimproved soils, would not need so much feeding. Those who have decided to garden, which is not nature's way, will have to give something back to the earth every year. Horticulture is an intensive business and in time even the best soils get exhausted, but there is no need to forgo organic principles.

Manure and home-made compost are far the best soil improvers. Blood, fish and bone is a good long-term fertilizer, and seaweed extracts are useful for a quick boost. All of these can be used with a clear conscience. Never apply any fertilizer directly to the leaves or to dry soil. There is no need to water it in: just wait for a rainy day.

WATERING

It is hard for us not to water on our fast-draining limestone soil. I would prefer not to do so, but plants suffer very quickly here in times of drought. Gardeners on similarly light soils who do not want the labour, or the ecological irresponsibility, of watering will find it difficult to grow fruit, vegetables or lush and greedy flowers. There are plenty of plants that would thrive, like Mediterranean shrubs, but I want to grow other things. These are the sort that, left unwatered, tend to be attacked by diseases and pests. Mildew appears on polemoniums, roses and pulmonarias as soon as the ground is dry. It is true that all well-grown plants succumb less easily to horticultural perils than those which are struggling for life, and that mulching and years of soil improvement help to reduce the need for water. When you plant, dig deep planting pits full of organic matter as they help to keep the ground moist.

OPPOSITE: *A garden that is uncherished always seem to lack life. Signs of work in progress make a place look occupied, as here.*

LEFT: *The fine spray of water on the flowers in this picture also indicates a loving owner, but here the practice suits the photographer better than the flowers. Watering in direct sunlight can cause leaves to become scorched and water to be wasted.*

throws the water as high and as far as possible to emulate gentle rain. The commercial models are beautiful and by far the best, but expensive.

PESTS

Vigilance is vital. If you can spot trouble early you can usually cure it without chemicals. A case of mildew on a herbaceous plant or a rose in early summer can often be repelled by water. If it is bad, cutting the plant down and watering it into new life will restore it in a few weeks. We almost never spray, but hand-held organic pest controls are sometimes used on the growing tips of roses if aphids are bad. If blackfly appears, as it invariably does on the golden elder, the shoots that carry it are pinched out immediately. In gardens where slugs and snails are bad, like this one, it is disheartening to see rows of seedlings eaten to the quick, so we do use slug pellets that are harmless to birds, a few at a time but often. In early spring, as the delphinium shoots come through, they are essential.

The worst pests here are much larger than insects. Birds descend on cabbages and wallflowers unless they are netted. Rabbits are everywhere in spite of walls and wire in what seem to be gaps. There is very little that can be done. Renardine, the disgusting foxy-smelling tar oil, keeps them away but the smell deters humans too. Peppering plants helps, but is not infallible. Cocooning them in wire as they emerge is another defence. If we did not do this to the crambe, until it has grown more than 30 centimetres high, rabbits would eat all the new growth. I am learning that some plants like pinks and soft-leaved campanulas are a waste of time in rabbit-infested areas. Others, like aquilegias, which have a reputation for being rabbit-proof, are also devoured, but if the plants are big enough when they go in, they can survive having all their lower leaves nibbled away. Mice and voles are not everyone's problem, but they are ours. Clematis and peach shoots, tulip and crocus bulbs and any form of pea or bean are their preferred foods. I have not found that dipping bulbs in paraffin, oil or petrol or planting them with a holly leaf works, but others swear by these methods. Traps are the only sure way to control mice, but be prepared to set several and to put each one in a place where it will not attract birds. Neither cats nor poison am I prepared to try, but others may find these

Seep hose, laid on the ground between plants, is much the most efficient and economical way of watering. Plants that need extra rations can be encircled with the pipe.

Where irrigation is essential, I recommend the porous hosepipe that we use in the hellebore beds and the church border; this is the most economical way of watering that I know. Those who can afford a length of this seep hose, made from recycled car tyres, could not spend their money more wisely. Laid along new hedges under a mulch, it will cut out hours of hand-held hoses in dry periods and will allow you to boost growth with added feeds of dried blood during the summer. I would avoid the kind of micro-irrigation system that has nozzles, as this tends to clog and is much more expensive to buy. Overhead sprinklers are also less efficient as they waste water, and on sunny days they cannot be used because they tend to scorch leaves. For the vegetables, we do use a sprinkler. Choose one that acceptable·options. In any garden there will always be predators. Learn to recognize them, then decide whether fight or flight is the best technique for you. The fight will be long and hard and you will probably not win, so outwitting them by removing the source of attraction either by nets or wire, or by enclosing the plants in a safe place may be the least demanding course of action.

PRUNING

Pruning is another inescapable annual job. All plants will grow without human intervention, but the aim of pruning is to keep the shrub manageable, as well as encouraging it to produce as many flowers as possible on your behalf. On any shrub (and this includes roses) all dead and spindly wood should be removed and efforts should be made to keep the middle of a bush open to sun and air, which means cutting out crossing shoots in the middle of a plant. You are also trying to reduce wind damage to the roots, so top-heavy plants will need to have their shoots shortened if they are waving about. Those are general rules which can be applied to all shrubs. You will need to look up how to prune what you buy, but as a rough guide, those plants which flower on the wood that they made the previous summer, like philadelphus and winter jasmine, will need to have all this cut away after flowering to allow maximum light and air for the shoots that will make the flowers in the following summer. But those which flower on the current year's growth, like roses, buddleja and ceanothus, must be pruned hard in early spring to encourage them to put out lots of flowering shoots. It may help to make your own pruning timetable which can be pinned on the wall where you keep your tools. Few people can remember to which group a particular clematis belongs: much of my early gardening life was spent going indoors to look up the difference between redcurrants and blackcurrants. In the winter, research a list of all those plants that you grow that need pruning and you will save yourself time in summer.

Roses on walls flower better if you can encourage their shoots to bend downwards. Shorten each tip and tie them in firmly to the wires (never poke them behind) in several places along the shoot, using tarred string, rather than wire. This can be done in autumn or winter, provided it is not frosty. They should cover the wall with roses

When pruning shrubs that flower on wood grown the previous summer, such as philadelphus, it is important to remove the old wood that has flowered as soon as flowering is over.

Buddleja flowers on wood made the same summer and requires hard pruning in late winter.

Lilacs need deadheading and can be rejuvenated slowly.

Roses trained to a wall do better if they can be made to curve. The side shoots are tipped and trained into any spaces left. It may also be necessary to remove one or two of the oldest main shoots each year.

Buddleja, like this spectacular bush of 'Dartmoor', need regular deadheading as they flower, or their appearance will be spoilt.

the following summer. Fruit trees that are grown in restricted forms, such as espaliered apples, will need summer pruning; so will wisterias.

CUTTING BACK PERENNIALS

The shearing of shrubs is well documented, but perennial plants respond to pruning too and this information is not so easy to find. From other gardeners, I have learned that early nipping of flowers like asters, chrysanthemums and phlox makes bushier plants and reduces the need for staking. Traditional delphiniums can be made to flower for longer if you cut back alternate stems on each plant, so that one half flowers earlier than the other. Or you can allow all the flowers to come at once, then cut the whole plant down,

feed it and water it and wait for an autumn crop. Many other herbaceous plants will give you a second flowering in a summer if you cut them down as they come to the end of their performance. Hardy geraniums, violas, polemoniums, centaureas, alchemilla and nepeta, to name a few, can all be encouraged to repeat their efforts. Violas literally flower themselves silly. Like children at a party, they go on until they end up bedraggled and exhausted. Cut them back as they show signs of looking seedy and they will revive in a matter of weeks to flower again just as hard as they did before. The timing of these operations varies from year to year, but if you watch the plants you will see when they start to slow down. Shear them off completely, feed them and water them and they will soon cheer up. Dead-heading,

Delphiniums can be made to stagger their flowers if alternate stems are cut back in early summer as this checks their growth.

When deadheading roses, prune them back to a new shoot otherwise the stalks will look ugly and will ultimately die back.

that favourite pastime of lady gardeners who never have dirty fingernails, is also a form of summer pruning. Most gardeners who grow roses tend to dead-head them by pulling off the dead flowers with finger and thumb. Cut back to a bud, they will have fewer unsightly snags and will flower for longer. Many other plants can be coaxed into an extended performance if they can be prevented from setting seed. Here, regular picking of Iceland poppies keeps them flowering for months, and favourite aquilegias can be kept going until well after midsummer. Barnhaven primulas, Scotch marigolds, hemerocallis, Shasta daisies, cornflowers, irises, scabious and pinks are some of the plants which I bother to dead-head. The garden looks better tended for it and the flowers last longer. If there were more time, I know that many more plants would respond to the same treatment. Seeding weakens plants, and mildew and botrytis are much more likely to strike if you allow plants to go to seed, so hellebores and peonies are healthier if the old flowering stems are cut out. You can save one or two flowers if you want them to set seed, but the rest are better taken off. Dead-heading and cutting back plants that are over keeps a garden looking fresh.

There are always difficult times, when the decision to cut down a plant on the wane must be taken. As each plant finishes in the summer garden I worry that there will be nothing to take its place, but when it comes to the moment of action, I find that I can remove barrow loads of spent flower stems without too many gaps appearing. Occasionally a plant has to be pulled across to fill a space, or we have to look for something to plant instead. A back-up of reserves in the narrow border under the north wall of the kitchen garden provides a useful source of fillers. We tend to grow extra tobacco plants and cosmos every year in case of such emergencies. Asters and chrysanthemums that have been divided in spring and lined out until they get bigger will always move easily. As a last resort, sometimes a pelargonium like 'Brunswick' can look just right in a gap. In the course of any summer, friends bring plants, or I see things that are irresistible, so a few spaces are always welcome. Prolonging the show is, I think, the hardest part of garden management. So many places look tired and over after the roses have faded, so planning for late summer is important. In recent years, warm autumn months have further extended the flowering season.

The point of staking is to give plants support, but it also allows you to grow more plants in a bed. Pea sticks can be woven together to make a firm but elastic surround for plants such as the peonies shown here. All the stakes need to be put in early in the year.

LEFT: *Delphiniums are easily snapped by the wind and always need support. This home-made frame is more obtrusive than pea sticks would have been, but so well done that it adds to the general effect.*

BELOW: *Light flowers, like the poppies, can stand alone. They are the easiest of flowers to raise from seed, but as they resent being transplanted they are better sown where they are to flower, or in pots.*

foxgloves, crambe and angelica are all reliable stalwarts. Watering and heavy rain will often lay low plants that ought to be able to stand on their own roots, but wind is the worst flattener of flowers that I know. As with every operation in the garden, thinking ahead is the best way to prevent trouble. If you garden in a windy place and cannot cope with staking, then you will need to plan borders with a self-supporting cast of flowers.

PROPAGATION

Behind the scenes, much of the work is optional. It is possible to run a garden without doing any propagation. If you are organized, you can arrange things so that you buy in plants of vegetables and tender bedding plants. If you are busy or short of space this is probably sensible and, if you cost your own labour, not too expensive. It is a pity though, because half the fun of gardening is raising your own plants and having so many that there are some to spare to give away. Here we grow too many biennials – foxgloves, wallflowers, sweet Williams, Iceland poppies, angelica, the white variegated honesty, *Salvia sclarea* var. *turkestanica* –

STAKING

Keeping plants upright is another technique to master if you want to show them at their best. Delphiniums, asters, peonies and perennial poppies, as well as many others, will need support. This is difficult and fiddly work. Good staking is an art because neither sticks nor string should be visible when the plant is fully grown. The best practitioners start early in the season. Once a plant has fallen over it is much harder to set it straight again. In winter, we gather sheaves of pea-sticks, but by the end of the summer there are never enough to go round. Lavish expenditure on ready-made stakes would be one solution to this problem, but they look less attractive and do not bend with the plants in the way that pea-sticks do. Smaller plants would be another option. If you lack the time or the inclination to prop plants up, it is probably better to shun the giants which will always need support. This need not mean forgoing delphiniums: the Belladonna hybrids are lovely plants and flower for longer than the overbearing dowagers of the herbaceous border. Not all the giants need a prop. Verbascums,

the list goes on. If I were short of time and space I know it would be better to give them up, but not yet. Taking cuttings of plants which need regular renewal, like violas and dianthus, or some of the half-hardy plants that may not survive the winter outside, is less demanding. Greenhouse work is delightful, but impossible to contemplate unless you never go away or have someone to stand in for you when you do. Pots too are a daily commitment in summer and not something to undertake if you cannot spare time to look after them properly. The important thing is to know what your limits are and stick to a work programme that you can achieve. Doing things at the right time is not essential, but can save time. If you hoe before the weeds appear and prune before the shrubs are out of control, life is easier. Management by crisis is not the best precept to adopt in a garden, so a couple of hours every two or three days is always better value than a once-a-month blitz. Never plan more than you are satisfied you can manage, but as the garden matures it will become easier. If it is a demanding chore, find ways of making it simple. Most important of all is that the garden should be a place of peace and relaxation.

ABOVE: *Growing biennials like the foxgloves above is always worthwhile and there is great satisfaction in raising plants from cuttings.*

BELOW: *Plastic lemonade bottles cut in half make good propagating units. The tops can be removed to let in air if necessary.*

FAVOURITE PLANTS

The plants on the following lists are personal favourites; the choice is not meant to be comprehensive. Given proper care and a good start, none of them is particularly demanding to grow. **T** means that a plant is tender, **B** that it has a tendency to be biennial, **S** that it is suitable for shade.

LINCHPIN PLANTS

The following is a selection of key plants that will define the style or character of a planting scheme, providing a year-round presence or a seasonal highlight around which to design the rest of the scheme.

For shape and foliage

Trees:
Crataegus laevigata 'Rosea
  Flore Pleno'
The pale pink double hawthorn makes a lovely fast-growing tree that is easy to grow in almost any conditions.
Magnolia x *soulangeana*
As useful for its snaky branches in winter as for its flowers in spring. In cold climates, pick the late-flowering form 'Lennei'.
Malus domestica
Apple trees are beautiful as well as useful. 'Discovery', 'Arthur Turner' and, where there is room, 'Bramley's Seedling' will all give a garden character. Insist on standards or half-standards. Modern bush forms will never make trees.
Malus transitoria
Small graceful crab apple.
Morus nigra
The black mulberry makes a beautiful shape quite early in life.
Prunus x *subhirtella*
  'Autumnalis'
Ask for the white and not the pink form ('Autumnalis Rosea') of this winter-flowering cherry. The white is out for much longer. Seen against an evergreen background in warm spells in winter, it is one of the thrills of the gardener's year.

Ptelea trifoliata
The Indian hop tree has tiny scented flowers, pretty leaves and green seed clusters.
Robinia x *slavinii* 'Hillieri'
A round-headed small acacia with elegant leaves and scented pink flowers in summer.

Large shrubs:
Buxus sempervirens
  (in various forms)
Green box gives shape and definition to any scheme and provides a winter presence.
Cotinus coggygria
  'Notcutt's Variety'
For those who like a purple centrepiece, this plum-coloured form of the smoke bush makes a good background for deep rich colours.
Ilex aquifolium 'Golden
  Queen', 'Silver Queen'
The variegated hollies brighten any garden in winter.
Mahonia x *media* 'Charity'
Huge evergreen leaves and yellow winter flowers.
Osmanthus delavayi
Tiny evergreen leaves and scented flowers in April. Not for cold gardens.
Rhamnus alaternus
  'Argenteovariegata'
This silvery-edged evergreen shrub from the Mediterranean looks good with roses.
Rosa glauca
The dusky glaucous-leaved shrub rose.
Sambucus racemosa
  'Plumosa Aurea'
The cut-leaved golden elder is better in partial shade than in sun.
Viburnum plicatum 'Mariesii'
A flat, tiered bush that carries dazzling white flowers.

Smaller plants with presence

Acanthus spinosus
The long divided leaves are the classical foliage found on Corinthian capitals. The form *spinosissimus* is even more finely carved, but not so hardy.
Alchemilla mollis
With calm round leaves and airy sprays of green flowers, it deserves its reputation as everybody's favourite. Cut back before it seeds.
Artemisia lactiflora 'Guizhou'
Pewter leaves tinged with pink. Tiny white flowers. A damp site is best.
Euphorbia characias subsp.
  wulfenii 'Lambrook Gold'
The best of the large euphorbias.
Euphorbia x *martinii*
Smaller than 'Lambrook Gold' and with red stems, this is an obliging plant.
Fuchsia magellanica var.
  gracilis 'Tricolor'
Pinky grey leaves all summer. S
Helleborus argutifolius
The Corsican hellebore has handsome leaves and green flowers for months.
Iris pallida var. *pallida*
The only iris that has respectable leaves all summer. Scented pale blue flowers.
Melianthus major
For hot places. The bluey grey foliage looks as though it has been carved, but their smell is not the leaves' best feature.
Morina longifolia
Pink thistle-like flowers.
Rosmarinus officinalis 'Miss
  Jessopp's Upright'
For hot dry places the upright rosemary makes columns of silvery green.

Long-flowering shrubs

Buddleja davidii 'Nanho Blue'
Evergreen leaves in mild winters, more delicate looking than most buddlejas.
Lavatera 'Barnsley'
Its pale pink flowers give a cheerful start to any new garden until the more distinguished plants are fully grown. The newer *Lavatera* 'Pink Frills' looks more unusual, with smaller flowers.

Roses

Many of the older types are suitable as a focus for the summer months. In large schemes the Hybrid Musks 'Buff Beauty', 'Penelope' and 'Felicia' always look settled.
Rosa 'Cerise Bouquet'
Flings out sprays of shocking pink flowers all summer on finely cut leaves. Very large.
Rosa 'De Rescht'
Crimson flowers in an old-fashioned shape which repeat throughout the summer on tidy bushes.
Rosa 'Pearl Drift'
A new rose which looks old-fashioned but has many modern qualities. Free-flowering, good leaves and low spreading habit with large white flowers.

Tall shrubs and perennials
(over 90 centimetres)

Anemone hupehensis
  'September Charm'
The pink Japanese anemones and the white (*A.* x *hybrida* 'Honorine Jobert') are lovely late summer features.

Dahlia 'Arabian Night'
Dahlias are invaluable late-summer performers and are substantial enough to be the key players in a planting. This deep crimson black is my favourite, but there is a huge colour range to choose from.
Delphinium x *belladonna*
These delphiniums do not usually need staking and flower for much longer than the traditional varieties. 'Völkerfrieden' is gentian blue, 'Moerheimii' creamy white and 'Cliveden Beauty' pale porcelain blue.
Nepeta 'Six Hills Giant'
The best and hardiest of the larger catmints. *N. sibirica* is equally tall but a paler blue. Both are in flower for months and will repeat after being cut back.
Verbena bonariensis
Airy tender perennial that flowers throughout late summer with deep purple, tiny heads on slim, rigid stems as tall as a man.

Smaller long-flowering sub-shrubs and perennials
(as repeated elements in a scheme these might qualify as linchpins)

Aster x *frikartii* 'Mönch'
The lavender-blue-flowered Michaelmas daisy is out for much of the summer after the roses have faded.
Aster lateriflorus 'Horizontalis'
Wiry bushes with pinkish stems and tiny daisies in autumn.
Erysimum 'Bowles' Mauve'
Still the most reliable and substantial of the perennial wallflowers, grey leaves and purple spikes almost all summer.
Erysimum 'Constant Cheer'
Green leaves and pinky russet flowers over a long season.
Gaura lindheimeri
Clouds of starry white flowers in late summer, succeeds best in well-drained, warm places.

PLANTS FOR DIFFERENT SEASONS

The lists below include many of the plants that I would be sorry to leave out of a garden. In one place or another I have grown them with pleasure and not too much trouble. It is worth insisting on the forms named. The timing of the appearance of the perennials and bulbs that follow the tree, shrub and climber lists will vary from season to season. Their sequence should not alter much. It is possible to control and delay some flowers by cutting plants back, or by dividing ones like the hardy geraniums in spring so that they start later and flower for longer. These tricks you will only discover by a process of trial and error. What works in some gardens will not invariably succeed everywhere. For plants that I recommend in numerous forms there are separate lists on p. 205. An asterisk denotes plants that carry on flowering into the next season.

Winter, early spring

Trees and shrubs:
Buxus sempervirens 'Elegantissima' **S**
Camellia 'Cornish Snow' **S**
Camellia x *williamsii* **S**
Chimonanthus fragrans
Cornus mas **S**
Daphne mezereum f. *alba* **S**
Garrya elliptica 'James Roof' **S**
Hamamelis x *intermedia* 'Pallida' **S**
Lonicera x *purpusii* 'Winter Beauty'
Mahonia japonica 'Bealei' **S**
Mahonia x *media* 'Charity' **S**
Pittosporum 'Garnettii'
Prunus x *subhirtella* 'Autumnalis'
Ribes laurifolium **S**
Sarcococca hookeriana var. *digyna* **S**

Viburnum x *bodnantense* 'Dawn' **S**
Viburnum farreri 'Farrer's Pink'
Viburnum tinus 'Eve Price' **S**
Viburnum tinus 'Lucidum' **S**

Climbers and wall shrubs:
Azara microphylla
Clematis armandii 'Apple Blossom' **S**
Clematis cirrhosa 'Freckles' **S**
Coronilla valentina subsp. *glauca* 'Citrina'*
Hedera helix 'Glacier' **S**
Hedera helix 'Goldheart' **S**
Hedera hibernica **S**
Jasminum nudiflorum **S**
Prunus mume 'Beni-chidori'
Prunus mume 'Omoi-no-mama'

Perennials and bulbs:
*Anemone blanda**
Bergenia 'Ballawley' **S**
Bergenia 'Silberlicht' **S**
Crocus biflorus subsp. *weldenii*
Crocus 'Blue Pearl'
Crocus 'Cream Beauty'
Crocus 'E.A. Bowles'
Crocus tommasinianus
Cyclamen coum
Eranthis hyemalis
Galanthus (see list, p. 205) **S**
Helleborus niger forms (see list, p. 205)
*Helleborus orientalis** (see list, p. 205) **S**
Iris 'Joyce'
Iris 'Katharine Hodgkin'
Iris unguicularis 'Mary Barnard'
Iris unguicularis 'Walter Butt'
Primula Cowichan Venetian Red polyanthus **S**
Primula Cowichan Blue polyanthus **S**
Pulmonaria officinalis 'Sissinghurst White' **S**
Pulmonaria rubra 'Redstart' **S**
Pulmonaria saccharata 'Frühlingshimmel' **S**
Pulmonaria saccharata 'Glebe Blue' **S**
Viola odorata **S**

Spring

Trees and shrubs:
Amelanchier lamarckii
Chaenomeles speciosa 'Moerloosei' **S**
Chaenomeles x *superba* 'Lemon and Lime' **S**
Chaenomeles x *superba* 'Rowallane' **S**
Crataegus laciniata
Daphne blagayana
Daphne odora 'Aureomarginata'
Daphne tangutica retusa
Forsythia suspensa 'Atrocaulis' **S**
Magnolia kobus **S**
Magnolia x *soulangeana* **S**
Osmanthus delavayi
Paeonia delavayi **S**
Prunus tenella
Ribes x *gordonianum* **S**
Ribes sanguineum 'Pulborough Scarlet' **S**
Ribes speciosum **S**
Syringa microphylla 'Superba' **S**
Viburnum x *burkwoodii* 'Park Farm Hybrid' **S**
Viburnum carlesii 'Aurora' **S**
Viburnum plicatum 'Pink Beauty' **S**

Climbers:
Clematis alpina 'Frances Rivis'
Clematis macropetala 'Maidwell Hall'
Clematis macropetala 'Markham's Pink'

Perennials and bulbs:
Brunnera macrophylla **S**
Cardamine pratensis 'Flore Pleno'
Chionodoxa
*Crocus**
Dianthus (see list, p. 205)
Dicentra 'Langtrees' **S**
Dicentra 'Stuart Boothman' **S**
Erysimum 'Bowles' Mauve'*
Erysimum 'Bredon'
Erysimum 'Constant Cheer'*
Erysimum 'John Codrington'*
Euphorbia characias subsp. *wulfenii* **S***
Euphorbia myrsinites
Euphorbia polychroma **S***
Galanthus (see list, p.205) **S**

Helleborus argutifolius S*
Helleborus foetidus forms*
 (see list, p. 205) S
Helleborus lividus S
Helleborus × *sternii* forms
 (see list, p.205) S
Iris bucharica
Iris (Intermediate Bearded)
 'Greenspot'
Iris (Standard Dwarf Bearded)
 'Austrian Sky'
Iris (Standard Dwarf Bearded)
 'Blue Hendred'
Iris (Standard Dwarf Bearded)
 'Clay's Caper'
Iris (Standard Dwarf Bearded)
 'Hocus Pocus'
Iris (Standard Dwarf Bearded)
 'Lemon Flare'
Iris (Standard Dwarf Bearded)
 'Little Blackfoot'
Muscari S
Narcissus Cyclamineus
 hybrids S
Narcissus 'February Gold'
Narcissus 'February Silver'
Narcissus 'Jenny'
Narcissus pseudonarcissus
 subsp. *obvallaris* S
Narcissus 'Thalia'
Paeonia cambessedesii
Phlox divaricata subsp.
 laphamii 'Chattahoochee'
Polemonium foliosissimum S
Polemonium 'Lambrook
 Mauve' S
Polemonium 'Sonia's Bluebell' S
Primula auricula (see list,
 p. 205)
Primula 'Corporal Baxter' S
Primula Cowichan polyanthus S
Primula 'Ken Dearman' S
Primula 'Tawny Port'
Primula vulgaris 'Alba Plena'
Primula 'Wanda' S
Pulmonaria 'Glebe Blue' S
Pulmonaria 'Lewis Palmer' S
Pulmonaria 'Mawson's Blue' S
Pulmonaria 'Weetwood Blue' S
Ranunculus aconitifolius 'Flore
 Pleno' S
Scilla siberica
Tulipa (see list, p. 205)
Vinca minor 'Atropurpurea' S
Vinca minor 'Gertrude Jekyll' S
Vinca minor 'La Grave' S
Viola odorata S

Late spring/early summer

Trees and shrubs:
Abutilon vitifolium var. *album*
Abutilon vitifolium 'Veronica
 Tennant'
Berberis × *ottawensis*
 'Superba' S
Buddleja alternifolia
Cistus × *cyprius*
Cistus × *hybridus*
 (syn. *C.* × *corbariensis*)
Cistus 'Peggy Sammons'
Cornus alba 'Elegantissima'
Hebe hulkeana
Magnolia wilsonii
Malus toringo subsp. *sargentii*
Philadelphus coronarius S
Prunus padus 'Watereri'
Prunus 'Shirotae'
Prunus 'Shogetsu'
Rubus 'Benenden' S
Syringa × *persica*
Syringa vulgaris 'Charles Joly' S
Syringa vulgaris 'Firmament' S
Syringa vulgaris 'Mme
 Lemoine' S
Syringa vulgaris 'Vestale' S
Weigela 'Florida Variegata' S
Weigela middendorffiana

Climbers:
Ceanothus 'Edinburgh'
Ceanothus 'Puget Blue'
Clematis montana 'Elizabeth' S
Hydrangea anomala subsp.
 petiolaris S
Lonicera periclymenum
 'Belgica'
Lonicera rupicola var.
 syringantha S
Lonicera × *tellmanniana* S
Schisandra rubriflora S
Wisteria floribunda 'Rosea'
Wisteria sinensis 'Alba'

Perennials and bulbs:
Allium giganteum
Allium hollandicum 'Purple
 Sensation'
Allium roseum
Anemone nemorosa
Angelica archangelica B S
Anthemis punctata subsp.
 cupaniana
Aquilegia chrysantha S
Aquilegia fragrans S

Aquilegia 'Hensol Harebell' S
Aquilegia Music series S
Aquilegia vulgaris 'Nivea' (syn.
 'Munstead White') S
Aubrieta 'Doctor Mules'
Bergenia ciliata
Centaurea montana
Convallaria majalis
Corydalis flexuosa 'China Blue' S
Dicentra 'Bacchanal' S
Dicentra spectabilis
Dicentra spectabilis 'Alba' S
Fritillaria imperialis
Fritillaria meleagris
Fritillaria pallidiflora
Geranium nodosum
Geranium phaeum S
Geranium sylvaticum
 'Mayflower' S
Geum 'Borisii'
Geum 'Mrs J. Bradshaw'
Helianthemum 'Henfield
 Brilliant'
Helianthemum 'The Bride'
Helianthemum 'Wisley
 Primrose'
Hemerocallis lilioasphodelus
Hesperis matronalis
Heuchera cylindrica
 'Greenfinch'
Iberis sempervirens
Iris (Border Bearded) 'Just
 Jennifer'
Iris graminea
Iris (Intermediate Bearded)
 'Avanelle'
Iris (Miniature Dwarf Bearded)
 'Adrienne Taylor'
Iris pallida var. *pallida*
Iris sibirica 'Cambridge'
Iris sibirica 'Flight of Butterflies'
Iris sibirica 'Orville Fay'
Iris sibirica 'Sparkling Rosé'
Iris (Tall Bearded) 'Annabel
 Jane'
Iris (Tall Bearded) 'Autumn
 Leaves'
Iris (Tall Bearded) 'Black Hills'
Iris (Tall Bearded) 'Deep
 Pacific'
Iris (Tall Bearded) 'Jane
 Phillips'
Iris (Tall Bearded) 'Lemon Tree'
Iris (Tall Bearded) 'Ruby Mine'
Lathyrus vernus
Leucojum aestivum S
Lunaria rediviva S

Lupinus arboreus
Muscari
Narcissus poeticus var. *recurvus* S
Nectaroscordon siculum
Nepeta 'Six Hills Giant'*
Paeonia delavayi
Paeonia mlokosewitschii S
Paeonia officinalis
Parahebe perfoliata
Primula Gold Laced
 polyanthus S
Primula 'Guinevere' S
Primula veris S
Primula vulgaris S
Pulsatilla vulgaris
Silene alpestris 'Flore Pleno'
Tulipa (see list, p. 205)
Veronica gentianoides
Viola 'Arkwright's Ruby' S
Viola 'Aspasia' S*
Viola 'Boughton Blue' S*
Viola cornuta 'Alba' S*
Viola 'Huntercombe Purple' S*
Viola 'Irish Molly' S
Viola 'Little David' S*
Viola 'Martin' S*
Viola 'Moonlight' S*
Viola 'Rebecca' S*

Midsummer

Trees and shrubs:
Bupleurum fruticosum S
Carpenteria californica
 'Ladhams' Variety'
Cytisus battandieri
Jasminum humile 'Revolutum'
Philadelphus 'Beauclerk' S
Philadelphus 'Belle Etoile' S
Potentilla fruticosa
 'Vilmoriniana'
Ptelea trifoliata
Roses (see list, p.205)
Santolina pinnata subsp.
 neapolitana 'Sulphurea'
Teucrium fruticans 'Azureum'
Viburnum opulus 'Roseum' S

Climbers:
Buddleja crispa
Jasminum officinale f. *affine*
Lathyrus latifolius 'White Pearl'
Lathyrus rotundifolius
Lonicera × *heckrottii*
 'Goldflame' S
Lonicera periclymenum
 'Serotina' S

Lonicera sempervirens **S**
Piptanthus nepalensis
Roses (see list, p. 205)
Solanum crispum 'Glasnevin'

Perennials and bulbs:
Alchemilla mollis **S**
Allium caeruleum
Allium cernuum
Allium christophii
Centranthus ruber
Cephalaria gigantea
Crambe cordifolia
Delphinium × *belladonna**
Dianthus (see list, p. 205)
*Erigeron karvinskianus**
Filipendula ulmaria 'Flore
  Pleno'
Geranium 'Ann Folkard'*
Geranium clarkei
  'Kashmir White'
Geranium himalayense
  'Gravetye'
Geranium 'Johnson's Blue'
Geranium macrorrhizum
  'Ingwersen's Variety'
Geranium × *oxonianum* 'A.T.
  Johnson' **S**
Geranium × *riversleaianum*
  'Mavis Simpson'*
Geranium × *riversleaianum*
  'Russell Prichard'*
Lupinus 'The Chatelaine'
Lupinus 'The Governor'
Nepeta sibirica 'Souvenir
  d'André Chaudron'
Paeonia lactiflora 'Duchesse
  de Nemours'
Paeonia lactiflora
  'Edulis Superba'
Paeonia lactiflora
  'Félix Crousse'
Paeonia lactiflora
  'Laura Dessert'
Paeonia lactiflora
  'Sarah Bernhardt'
Paeonia lactiflora 'White Wings'
Papaver orientale 'Cedric
  Morris'
Papaver orientale 'Turkish
  Delight'
Phlox 'Bill Baker'
Potentilla atrosanguinea
Potentilla 'Gibson's Scarlet'
Potentilla 'Monsieur Rouillard'
Potentilla nepalensis 'Miss
  Willmott'

Selinum wallichianum
  (syn. *S. tenuifolium*)
Verbascum chaixii 'Album' **B**
Verbascum 'Cotswold Queen' **B**
Verbascum 'Gainsborough' **B**
Verbascum 'Helen Johnson' **B**

Late summer

Trees and shrubs:
Artemisia abrotanum
Brachyglottis 'Sunshine'
Buddleja davidii 'Dartmoor'
Buddleja davidii 'Empire Blue'
Buddleja davidii 'Nanho Blue'*
Buddleja fallowiana var. *alba*
Buddleja lindleyana
Buddleja 'Pink Delight'
Ceanothus × *burkwoodii*
Clematis heracleifolia var.
  davidiana 'Wyevale'*
Clematis integrifolia
Escallonia 'Iveyi'
Hydrangea aspera villosa **S**
Hydrangea macrophylla
  'Mariesii Perfecta' (syn.
  'Blue Wave') **S**
Hydrangea macrophylla
  'Tricolor' **S**
Hydrangea 'Mme Emile
  Mouillère' **S***
Hydrangea quercifolia **S**
Hydrangea 'Preziosa' **S**
Lavandula angustifolia
  'Hidcote'*
Lavandula stoechas
Ligustrum lucidum **S**
Ligustrum quihoui **S**
Phygelius aequalis 'Yellow
  Trumpet'*
Phygelius × *rectus* 'Winchester
  Fanfare'*
(Roses, see list, p.205)
Salvia microphylla var. *neurepia*

Climbers and wall shrubs:
Abelia × *grandiflora* 'Francis
  Mason'
Aconitum volubile **S**
Clematis 'Alba Luxurians' **S**
Clematis 'Bill Mackenzie' **S**
Clematis 'Duchess of Albany' **S**
Clematis 'Gravetye Beauty' **S**
Clematis 'Perle d'Azur' **S**
Clematis rehderiana **S**
Dicentra scandens
Lathyrus grandiflorus

Lonicera × *americana* **S**
Lonicera periclymenum
  'Graham Thomas' **S**
Myrtus communis
Passiflora caerulea
(Roses, see list, p. 205)
Trachelospermum jasminoides
Tropaeolum speciosum

Perennials and bulbs:
Acanthus mollis **S**
Acanthus spinosus **S**
Achillea 'Moonshine'
Achillea 'Schwefelblüte'
  ('Flowers of Sulphur')
Aconitum carmichaelii
  'Barker's Variety' **S**
Aconitum 'Ivorine' **S**
Aconitum 'Spark's Variety' **S**
Agapanthus Headbourne
  Hybrids
Alcea rosea 'Nigra' **B**
Alcea rugosa **B**
Allium sphaerocephalon
Anaphalis triplinervis
*Anemone hupehensis**
Artemisia lactiflora 'Guizhou'
Aster × *frikartii* 'Mönch'*
Campanula lactiflora 'Prichard's
  Variety' **S**
Campanula latiloba 'Hidcote
  Amethyst' **S**
Clematis × *durandii*
Coreopsis verticillata
  'Moonbeam'
Crocosmia 'Emily Mackenzie'
Crocosmia 'Lucifer'
Crocosmia 'Solfaterre'
Dahlia 'Arabian Night'*
Dahlia 'Bishop of Llandaff'*
Dahlia 'Claire de Lune'*
*Dahlia coccinea**
Dahlia 'Glorie van
  Heemstede'*
Dahlia 'Hugh Mather'*
Dahlia 'John Street'*
*Dahlia merckii**
Dahlia 'Moonlight'*
Dahlia 'Porcelain'*
Echinops bannaticus
  'Taplow Blue'
Epilobium angustifolium
  f. *album* **S**
Eryngium × *oliverianum*
Eryngium × *tripartitum*
Galega officinalis
*Gaura lindheimeri**

Geranium pratense 'Mrs
  Kendall Clark'
Geranium pratense 'Plenum
  Violaceum'
Geranium psilostemon
Geranium sanguineum var.
  striatum
Hemerocallis fulva 'Stafford' **S**
Hemerocallis 'Hyperion' **S**
Hemerocallis 'Marion
  Vaughn' **S**
Hemerocallis 'Whichford' **S**
Hosta plantaginea
Knautia macedonica
Kniphofia 'Green Jade'
Kniphofia 'Little Maid'
Leucanthemum × *superbum*
Lilium regale
Lobelia 'Queen Victoria' **T**
Lobelia tupa **T**
Lychnis coronaria 'Alba'
Lychnis coronaria
  'Atrosanguinea'
Macleaya microcarpa 'Kelway's
  Coral Plume'
Nepeta govaniana **S**
Nicotiana langsdorffii **T S**
Nicotiana sylvestris **T S**
Oenothera stricta
  'Sulphurea' **S***
Origanum laevigatum 'Hopleys'
Penstemon 'Evelyn'*
Penstemon 'Garnet'*
Phlox maculata 'Omega' **S**
Physostegia virginiana
  'Summer Snow'
Romneya coulteri
Salvia involucrata
  'Bethellii' **T***
Salvia sclarea var.
  turkestanica **B**
Salvia uliginosa **T**
Sedum 'Ruby Glow'
Sidalcea 'Elsie Heugh'
Tender perennials (see list)
Thalictrum delavayi
  'Hewitt's Double'
Thalictrum flavum
Verbascum olympicum **B**
Verbena bonariensis **T**

Autumn

Trees and shrubs:
Arbutus unedo **S**
Caryopteris × *clandonensis*
  'Heavenly Blue'

Ceratostigma willmottianum
Euonymus europaeus
  'Red Cascade' S
Euonymus hamiltonianus S
Eupatorium ligustrinum
Fuchsia magellanica var.
  molinae 'Sharpitor' S
Fuchsia magellanica
  'Versicolor' S
Fuchsia 'Riccartonii' S
Rosa moyesii
Rosa rugosa 'Alba'
Sorbus hupehensis
Viburnum opulus
  'Compactum' S
Viburnum opulus
  'Xanthocarpum' S
Viburnum plicatum
  'Nanum Semperflorens' S

Climbers:
Abutilon 'Kentish Belle'
Aconitum hemsleyanum
Campsis × *tagliabuana*
  'Mme Galen'
Ceanothus 'Autumnal Blue'
Cotoneaster horizontalis S
Dicentra scandens
Parthenocissus henryana S
Vitis 'Brant'
Vitis coignetiae

Perennials and bulbs:
Aconitum 'Bressingham Spire' S
Aster amellus 'King George'
Aster 'Coombe Fishacre'
Aster lateriflorus 'Horizontalis'
Aster 'Little Carlow'
Aster thomsonii 'Nanus'
Dendranthema 'Anastasia'
Dendranthema 'Clara Curtis'
Dendranthema 'Duchess
  of Edinburgh'
Dendranthema 'Emperor
  of China'
Dendranthema 'Mary Stoker'
Dendranthema 'Mei-kyo'
Dendranthema 'Wedding Day'
Geranium wallichianum
  'Buxton's Variety'
Nerine bowdenii
Salvia microphylla var.
  neurepia
Salvia uliginosa
Schizostylis coccinea 'Sunrise'
Schizostylis coccinea
  'Viscountess Byng'

BIENNIALS

*The biennials are a group of
plants that I find difficult to
ignore. They are hard work,
but many of these will last for
a second season and most will
reseed themselves. Some are
really perennials but are better
treated as biennials.*

Alcea rosea (singles) and 'Nigra'
Alcea rugosa
Angelica archangelica
Bellis perennis 'Pomponette'
Delphinium staphisagria
Dianthus barbatus auricula-
  eyed strains
Digitalis purpurea f. *albiflora*
Digitalis purpurea 'Sutton's
  Apricot' S
Erysimum 'Carmine Bedder'
Erysimum 'Primrose Bedder'
Erysimum 'Vulcan'
Lunaria annua 'Alba
  Variegata' S
Myosotis
Onopordum acanthium
Papaver nudicaule 'Constance
  Finnis'
Salvia sclarea var. *turkestanica*
Silybum marianum
Smyrnium perfoliatum S

ANNUALS

For quick impact

Antirrhinum 'Black Prince'
Borago officinalis
Calendula Art Shades
Centaurea cyanus
  (tall blue strains)
Cleome hassleriana
  'Helen Campbell'
Cosmos 'Purity'
Cosmos 'Versailles Red'
Helianthus annuus
  'Italian White'
Helianthus annuus
  'Velvet Queen'
Linum grandiflorum 'Rubrum'
Malva sylvestris 'Zebrina'
Nicotiana alata
Nicotiana langsdorffii
Nicotiana 'Lime Green'
Nicotiana sylvestris

Nigella damascena 'Miss Jekyll'
Papaver rhoeas (Shirley strains)
Papaver somniferum
  (peony-flowered)
Tropaeolum 'Empress of India'
Zinnia 'Envy'

Half-hardy annuals

*The following are good for
filling gaps or pots, but may
not survive the winter unless
precautions are taken.
Sometimes, with a mulch and
a mild winter, they will survive,
but it is safer to take cuttings
and bring them indoors.*

Anisodontea capensis
Argyranthemum gracile
  'Chelsea Girl'
Argyranthemum 'Vancouver'
Azorina vidalii (syn.
  Campanula vidallii)
Bidens ferulifolia
Convolvulus sabatius
Diascia lilacina
Diascia 'Ruby Field'
Francoa sonchifolia
Geranium palmatum
Heliotropium 'Chatsworth'
Heliotropium 'Princess Marina'
Lobelia 'Queen Victoria'
Lobelia tupa
Lotus berthelotii
Malva sylvestris 'Primley Blue'
Malvastrum lateritium
Mimulus glutinosus
(Scented leaf) *Pelargonium*
  (see list, p. 205)
Penstemon 'Apple Blossom'
Penstemon 'Blackbird'
Penstemon 'Catherine
  de la Mare'
Penstemon 'Evelyn'
Penstemon 'Garnet'
Penstemon 'Hidcote Pink'
Penstemon 'Rubicundus'
Penstemon 'Stapleford Gem'
Rhodanthemum gayanum
Salvia cacaliifolia
Salvia patens
Salvia uliginosa
Senecio cineraria
Sphaeralcea munroana
Tweedia caerulea
Verbena 'Apple Blossom'

Climbers:
Cobaea scandens 'Alba'
Eccremocarpus scaber
  (red and gold forms)
Ipomoea 'Heavenly Blue'
Lathyrus 'Noel Sutton'
Lathyrus odoratus
  (old-fashioned forms)
Rhodochiton atrosanguineus

FOLIAGE PLANTS

(for sun, with insignificant or
no flowers; many of these
are herbs)

Artemisia 'Powis Castle'
Ballota pseudodictamnus
Foeniculum vulgare 'Giant
  Bronze'
Hebe rakaiensis S
Lotus hirsutus (syn. *Dorycnium
  hirsutum*)
Origanum vulgare 'Aureum' S
Ruta graveolens
  'Jackman's Blue'
Salvia officinalis 'Icterina'
Salvia officinalis 'Purpurascens'
Salvia officinalis 'Tricolor'
Stachys byzantina
Thymus × *citriodorus*
  'Silver Queen'

*In shadier places try ferns. I
have found the following good,
even in fairly dry soil.*

Dryopteris filix-mas
Polypodium vulgare
Polystichum setiferum
  'Divisilobum'

PLANTS TO COLLECT

*The following plants are of
special interest to me. Roses,
hellebores, dianthus, tulips,
galanthus, auriculas and
pelargoniums are all flowers I
particularly enjoy. The choice
represents a nucleus of
favourites. I have never gardened
for long periods on damp soil
so I have less experience of
primulas, but would love to be
able to grow them better. These,
as well as dahlias, clematis,*

hardy geraniums, asters and
hardy chrysanthemums, are
also possible candidates for
future collections.

Auriculas
(best grown in pots and kept in
an airy frame in winter; shade)
 'Adrian'
 'Blue Steel'
 'Bonnard's Green'
 'Elsie'
 'Gretna Green'
 'Jack Dean'
 'Joy'
 'Lockyer's Gem'
 'Moneymoon'
 'Prague'
 'Rosebud'
 'Sandwood Bay'
 'Sirius'
 'St Boswells'
 'Susan'
 'Victor Bell'

Dianthus
(many are repeat-flowering)
 'Allspice'
 'Bat's Double Red'
 'Becky Robinson'
 'Brympton Red'
 'Farnham Rose'
 'Gran's Favourite'
 'Haytor White'
 'Inchmery'
 'Laced Monarch'
 'London Lovely'
 'Old Square Eyes'
 'Old Velvet'
 'Pike's Pink'
 'Queen of Sheba'
 'Red Emperor'
 'Red Welsh'
 'Rose de Mai'

Galanthus
(light shade)
 'Atkinsii'
 caucasicus
 'Desdemona'
 elwesii
 'Galatea'
 gracilis
 'Hippolyta'
 'Lady Beatrix Stanley'
 transcaucasicus
   (syn. G. lagodechianus)

'Magnet'
'Merlin'
nivalis
'Ophelia'
plicatus subsp. byzantinus
'S. Arnott'
'Straffan'
'Viradapicis'

Hellebores
 argutifolius
 atrorubens
 foetidus 'Green Giant'
 foetidus 'Miss Jekyll'
 foetidus 'Sopron'
 foetidus 'Wester Flisk'
 niger Blackthorn Group
 niger 'White Magic'
 × nigercors
 × nigristern
 orientalis subsp. abchasicus
   'Early Purple'
 orientalis Ashwood Strains
 orientalis 'Ballard's Black'
 orientalis 'Elizabeth
   Strangman's Pink'
 orientalis subsp. guttatus
 orientalis 'Yellow Ballard'
 × sternii Blackthorn Group
 × sternii 'Boughton Beauty'
 Torquatus hybrids

Pelargoniums
(can be brought inside in
winter, to stand on a
sunny sill)
 'Arden'
 'Barbe Bleu'
 'Brunswick'
 'Clorinda'
 'Copthorne'
 'Crimson Unique'
 crispum 'Variegatum'
 'Crystal Palace Gem'
 'Friesland'
 'Grey Lady Plymouth'
 'Lady Mary'
 'Lord Bute'
 'Miss Australia'
 'Mr Wren'
 'Mystery'
 'Paton's Unique'
 'Rollisson's Unique'
 'Sweet Mimosa'
 tomentosum
 'Vestale'
 'Yale'

Roses
 'Aloha'
 'Ballerina'
 'Buff Beauty'
 'Cardinal Hume'
 'Cécile Brunner'
 'Céleste'
 'Cerise Bouquet'
 'Complicata'
 'Comte de Chambord'
 'Cornelia'
 'De Rescht'
 'Dupontii'
 'Fantin-Latour'
 'Felicia'
 'Ferdinand Pichard'
 'Fru Dagmar Hastrup'
 'Fritz Nobis'
 'Frühlingsgold'
 glauca
 'Graham Thomas'
 'Heritage'
 'Iceberg'
 'Ispahan'
 'Jacques Cartier'
 'L.D. Braithwaite'
 'Maigold'
 'Mme Isaac Pereire'
 moyesii 'Geranium'
 'Nevada'
 nutkana 'Plena'
 'Pax'
 'Pearl Drift'
 'Penelope'
 'Petite de Hollande'
 pimpinellifolia 'Grandiflora'
 primula
 'Reine des Violettes'
 'Rose d'Amour'
 'Rosemary Rose'
 'Roseraie de l'Haÿ'
 'The Fairy'
 'White Pet'
 'Wickwar'
 'William Lobb'
 'Windrush'
 xanthina 'Canary Bird'
 xanthina f. hugonis
 'Yellow Button'
 'Yesterday'

Climbers
 'Adélaïde d'Orléans'
 'Albéric Barbier'
 'Albertine'
 'Alchymist'
 'Alister Stella Gray'

banksiae 'Lutea'
'Blush Noisette'
Climbing 'Pompon de Paris'
'Félicité Perpétue'
'Gloire de Dijon'
'Guinée'
'Leverkusen'
'Mermaid'
'Mme Alfred Carrière'
'New Dawn'
× odorata 'Mutabilis'
'Phyllis Bide'
'Rambling Rector'
'Sanders' White Rambler'
'Sombreuil'
'Zéphirine Drouhin'

Tulips
 'Abu Hassan'
 acuminata
 'Aladdin'
 'Angélique'
 'Apricot Beauty'
 'Apricot Parrot'
 'Artist'
 'Bleu Aimable'
 'Bright Eyes'
 'Carnaval de Nice'
 'China Pink'
 clusiana
 'Couleur Cardinal'
 'Estella Rijnveld'
 'Fantasy'
 'Flair'
 'Garden Party'
 'Generaal de Wet'
 'Hummingbird'
 linifolia (Batalinii group)
   'Bright Gem'
 'Marilyn'
 marjolettii
 'Maureen'
 'Maytime'
 'Orange Favourite'
 'Prince Charles'
 'Prince of Austria'
 'Purissima'
 'Queen of the Night'
 'Queen of Sheba'
 'Rococo'
 'Shirley'
 'Spring Green'
 sylvestris
 'Union Jack'
 'West Point'
 'White Triumphator'
 'Yokohama'

Index

Page numbers in italic refer to the illustrations. The list of Favourite Plants on pages 200–205 has not been included in the index.

ACKNOWLEDGEMENTS

Author's Acknowledgements

The list of those who have provided practical help, advice or plants (sometimes all three) throughout the making of this garden and the book will never, like the garden, be complete. At the time of writing, I want especially to thank the following: Nell Maydew, John Rimes, Des Hall, Tony Bowman, Dick Warriner, Sue Dickinson, Graham Harvey, John Sales, Ruth Birchall, Chloe Darling, Carole Clement, Corinne Renow-Clarke, Sarah Pearce, Louise Simpson, Stuart Cooper, Sarah Riddell, Jess Walton, Leslie Harrington, Lesley Craig and Tony Lord.

Picture Acknowledgements

14–15 Courtesy of Knight, Frank; 156–157 Andrew Lawson (Bramdean House, Hampshire); 158 Jill Mead (Greys Court, Oxfordshire); 159 Jill Mead (Mirabel Osler); 160 Marianne Majerus (Beth Chatto); 161 Clive Nichols (Le Manoir Aux Quat Saisons); 162 Jerry Harpur (Stonecrop, Coldspring, New York); 163 Jerry Harpur (Eastgrove Cottage Garden, Sankyns Green, Worcester); 164 Marianne Majerus (Mirabel Osler); 165 Ken Druse; 166 Marianne Majerus (Designer: Mark Brown); 167 *below* Ken Druse; 167 *above right* Marijke Heuff (La Casella); 167 *above left* Andrew Lawson (Private garden, Northamptonshire/Designer: Dan Pearson); 168 Marijke Heuff; 169 *above* Ken Druse (Designer: Margaret Roach); 169 *below* Marijke Heuff; 171 *above* Country Life/Hugh Palmer (Badminton); 171 *below* Gary Rogers; 172 Marianne Majerus; 174 *above* Marijke Heuff; 174 *below* Marijke Heuff (The Coach House, Oxfordshire); 175 S&O Mathews; 176 Clive Nichols (Wollerton Old Hall, Shropshire); 177 *below* Andrew Lawson (Ashtree Cottage, Wiltshire); 177 *above* Gary Rogers; 178 Richard Felber (Pam Kay, Ogunguit, Maine); 179 *above* Country Life/Anne Hyde (Hardwick Hall); 179 *below* Juliette Wade (The Old Chapel, Gloucestershire); 180 Clive Nichols (Hadspen Gardens, Somerset); 184 Country Life/Clive Boursnell (Barford Park); 185 Country Life/Alex Ramsay (Overbecks); 186 Henk Dijkman; 187 Marijke Heuff; 188 Jerry Harpur (Great Dixter, Northiam, Sussex); 189 Marijke Heuff (Boogaard); 190 Marijke Heuff (Ineke Greve); 191 *left* Marie O'Hara (Mr and Mrs Hinton); 191 *right* Maggie Oster (Dickey); 192 Jill Mead (Arden Hall, North Yorkshire); 193 Marijke Heuff (Brinkhof); 196 Neil Campbell-Sharp (Newby Hall); 198 *left* Jerry Harpur (Holker Hall, Grange-over-Sands, Cumbria); 198 *right* Steve Robson (Courtesy of John Morley); 199 Steve Robson (Pemberton Garden)

All other photographs by Andrew Lawson

Pinboard Acknowledgements

THE GOOSEBERRY GARDEN: 28–29
1 Clive Nichols (Chateau De Villandry, France); 2 Gemma Nesbitt (John & Carol Hubbard); 3 Angelo Hornak; 4 Mary Evans Picture Library; 5 The Natural History Museum, London/Bridgeman Art Library; 6 Clive Nichols (Chateau de Villandry, France); 7 C.S. Sykes/Interior Archive; 8 Andrew Lawson (Barnsley House)

THE POOL: 40–41
1 C.S. Sykes/Interior Archive; 2 Andrew Lawson (Knightshayes, Devon) 3 Country Life/Anne Hyde (Hardwick Hall, Derbyshire); 4 National Trust Picture Library/Nick Meers (Hidcote, Gloucestershire); 5 Tania Midgley; 6 Hugh Palmer (Knightshayes, Devon); 7 Marijke Heuff

THE DELL: 42–43
1 J.S. Sira/GPL; 2 Jerry Harpur (Writtle College, Essex); 3 John Glover/GPL; 4 Jerry Harpur (Newby Hall, Yorkshire); 5 Jerry Harpur; 6 Stephen Robson (Courtesy of Mr and Mrs Mullins, Pinbury Park); 7 Andrew Lawson; 8 Jerry Harpur (Benington Lordship, Hertfordshire)

THE KITCHEN GARDEN: 54–55
1 Sue Snell; 2 Brigitte Thomas/GPL; 3 Edifice/Weideger (West Dean, Sussex); 4 Sue Snell; 5 Sue Snell; 6 SIP/Yves Duronsoy; 7 Fine Art Photographic; 8 Mary Evans Picture Library; 9 Sue Snell

THE ORCHARD: 76–77
1 C.S. Sykes/Interior Archive; 2 Clive Nichols (Eastgrove Cottage, Hereford and Worcester); 3 Musee d'Orsay, Paris/Giraudon/ Bridgeman Art Library; 4 Sue Snell; 5 Andrew Lawson; 6 Photograph by James Ravilious/Common Ground; 7 Clay Perry/GPL; 8 Galleria Degli Uffizi, Florence/Bridgeman Art Library; 9 Courtesy of the Board of Trustees of the Victoria & Albert Museum, London/Bridgeman Art Library; 10 Courtesy of the Board of Trustees of the Victoria & Albert Museum, London

THE TERRACE: 88–89
1 Andrew Lawson (Beckley Park, Oxfordshire); 2 Andrew Lawson (Sapperton, Gloucestershire); 3 Country Life/Alex Ramsay (Plas Brondanw, Gwynedd); 4 Hugh Palmer (Beckley Park, Oxfordshire); 5 Robert Emmett Bright (Villa La Pietra Di Harold Acton); 6 Vivian Russell (Levens Hall, Cumbria); 7 Hugh Palmer (Hasely Court, Oxfordshire); 8 Marianne Majerus/GPL; 9 Andrew Lawson (Sapperton, Gloucestershire)

THE HELLEBORE BEDS: 98–99
1 National Trust Picture Library/Andrew Lawson; 2 Hugh Palmer (Essex House); 3 Courtesy of the Trustees of the Victoria & Albert Museum, London/Bridgeman Art Library; 4 John Glover/GPL; 5 Anne Hyde; 6 Andrew Lawson (The Old Rectory, Burghfield); 7 Anne Hyde; 8 Mary Evans Picture Library; 9 Anne Hyde; 10 Andrew Lawson (Kidlington, Oxfordshire); 11 Angelo Hornak

THE SUMMER AND WINTER GARDEN: 116–117
1 The Royal Horticultural Society, The Lindley Library; 2 Galerie George/Fine Art Photographic; 3 Harris Museum & Art Gallery, Preston, Lancashire/Bridgeman Art Library; 4 Fine Art Photographic; 5 National Trust Photographic Library/Nick Meers (Snowshill Manor); 6 The Royal Horticultural Society, The Lindley Library; 7 John Glover/GPL (Designer: Dan Pearson); 8 Angelo Hornak

THE CLIMBERS AND POTS: 136–137
1 Angelo Hornak; 2 City of Bristol Musuem & Art Gallery/Bridgeman Art Library; 3 Marianne Majerus; 4 Private Collection/Bridgeman Art Library; 5 Painting by John Morley; 6 Andrew Lawson; 7 Clive Nichols; 8 Sue Snell